JOURNALS INK.

WWW.FACEBOOK.COM/JOURNALSINK

COPYRIGHT © 2019 JOURNALS INK.

ALL RIGHTS RESERVED. NO PORTION OF THIS BOOK MAY BE REPRODUCED IN ANY FORM WITHOUT PERMISSION FROM THE PUBLISHER, EXCEPT AS PERMITTED BY U.S. COPYRIGHT LAW.

- REVIEWS -

YOUR THOUGHTS AND REVIEWS ARE ALWAYS APPRECIATED ON AMAZON, JUST - ONE OR TWO LINES IS HELPFUL

THANK YOU - ENJOY THE BOOK!

PUZZLE 5
BEGINNER

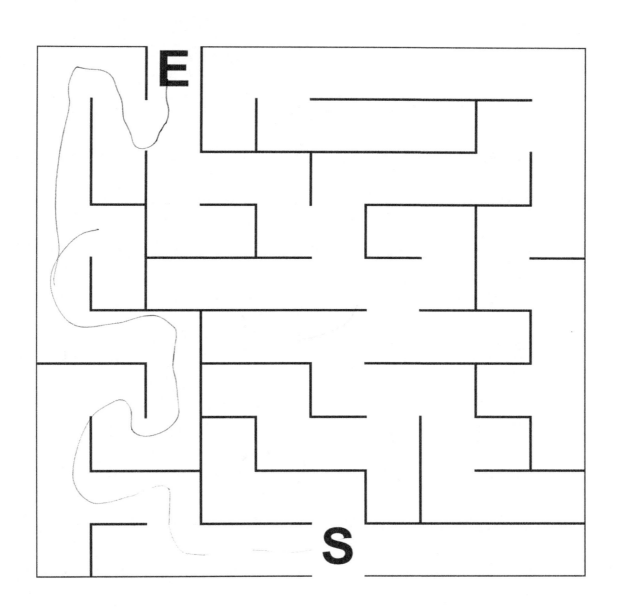

PUZZLE 6
BEGINNER

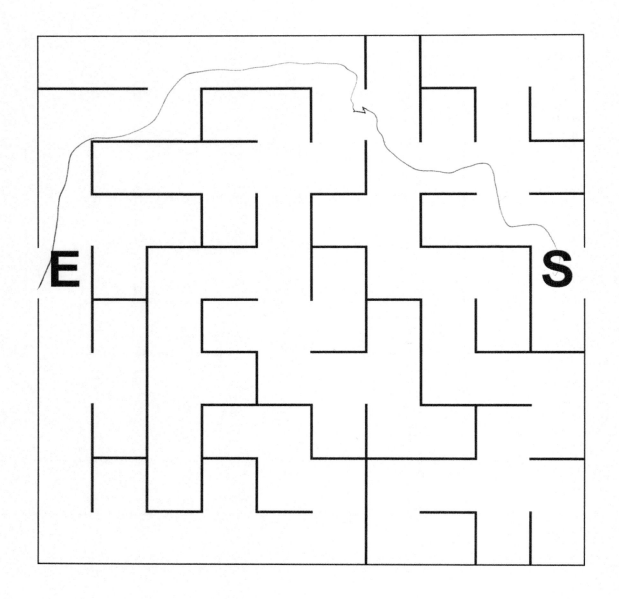

PUZZLE 11
BEGINNER

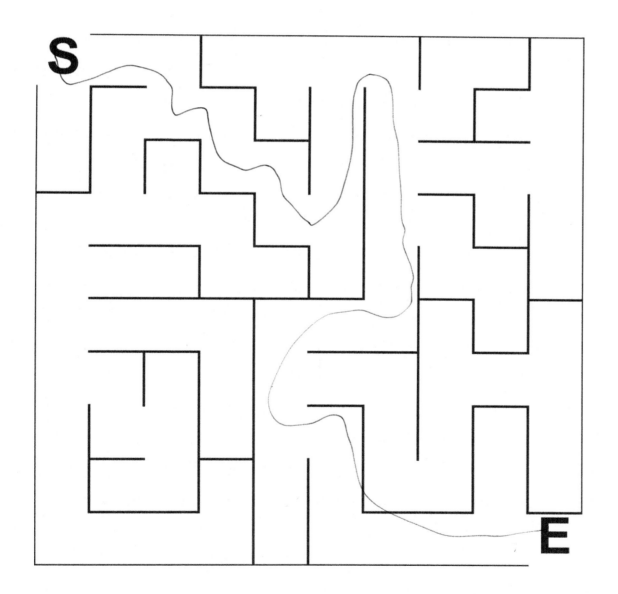

PUZZLE 12
BEGINNER

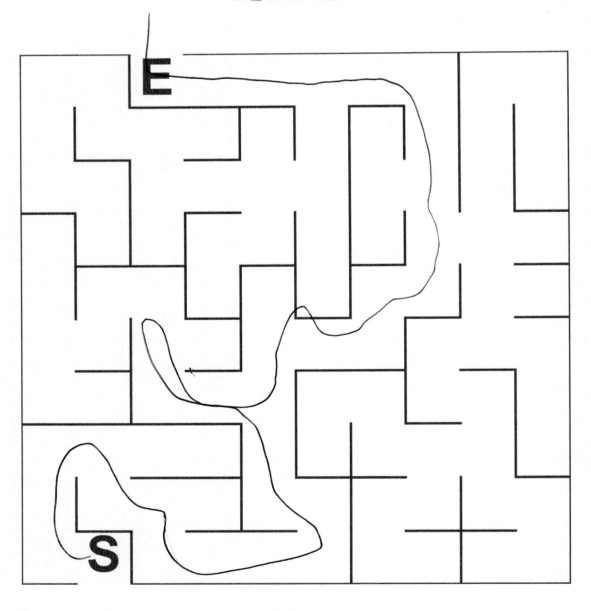

PUZZLE 13
BEGINNER

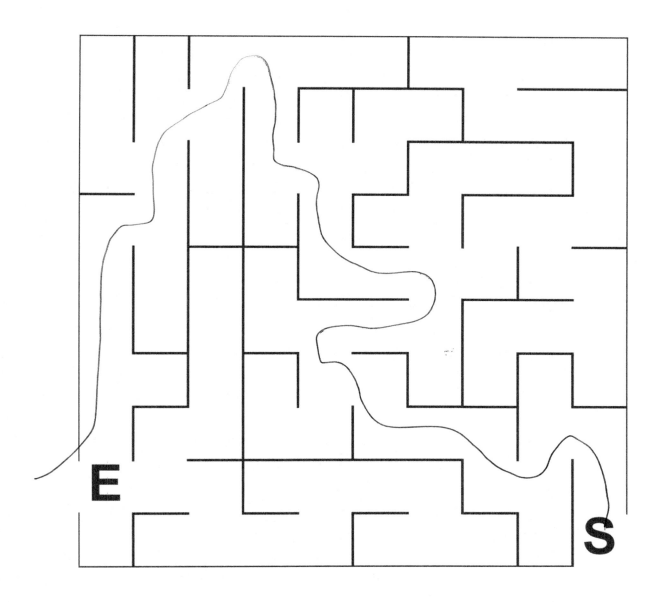

PUZZLE 14
BEGINNER

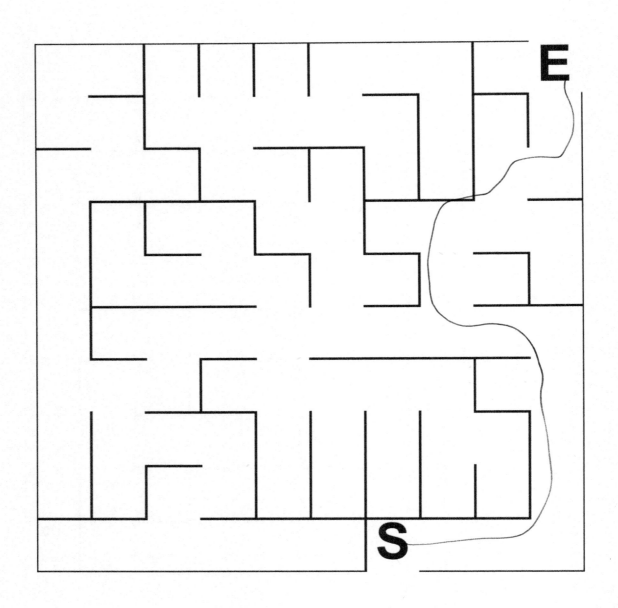

PUZZLE 15
BEGINNER

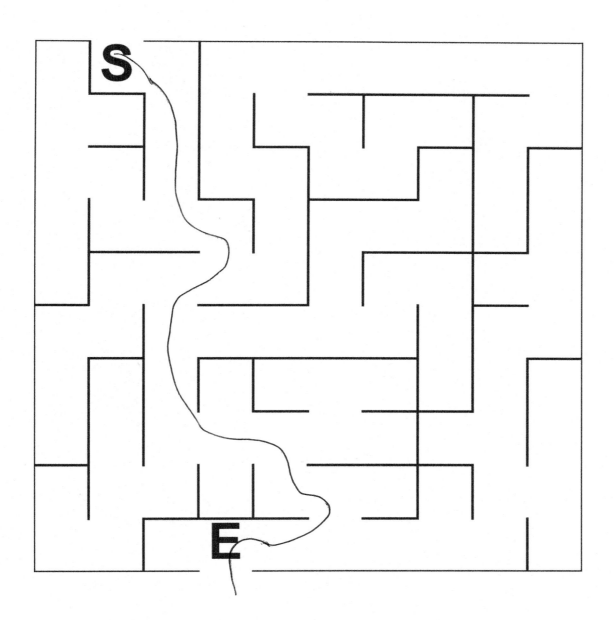

PUZZLE 23
SERIOUS

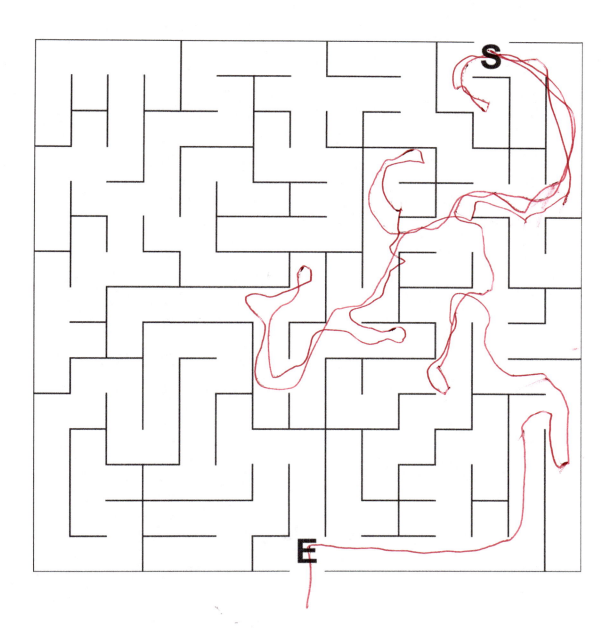

PUZZLE 25
SERIOUS

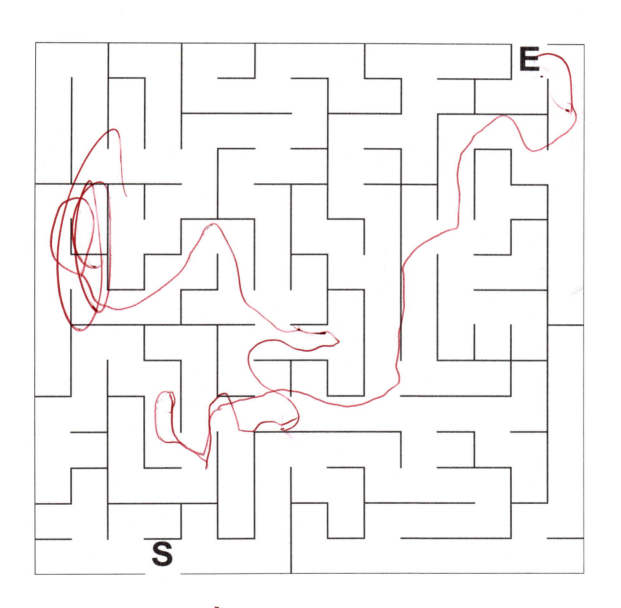

PUZZLE 26
SERIOUS

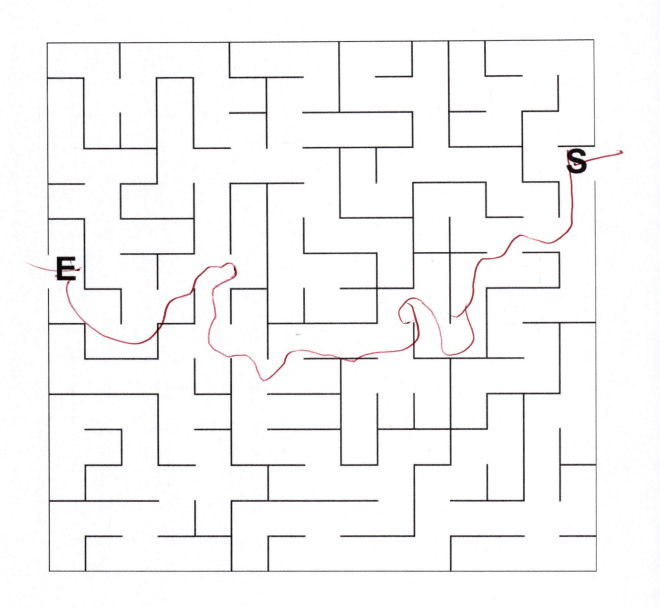

PUZZLE 35
SERIOUS

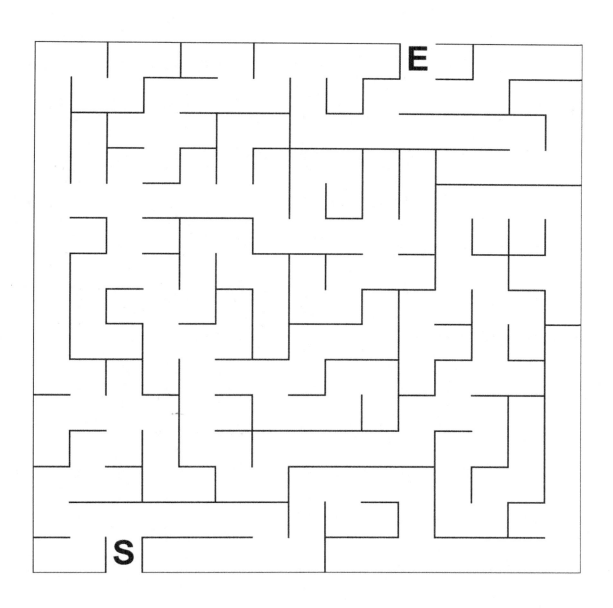

PUZZLE 36
SERIOUS

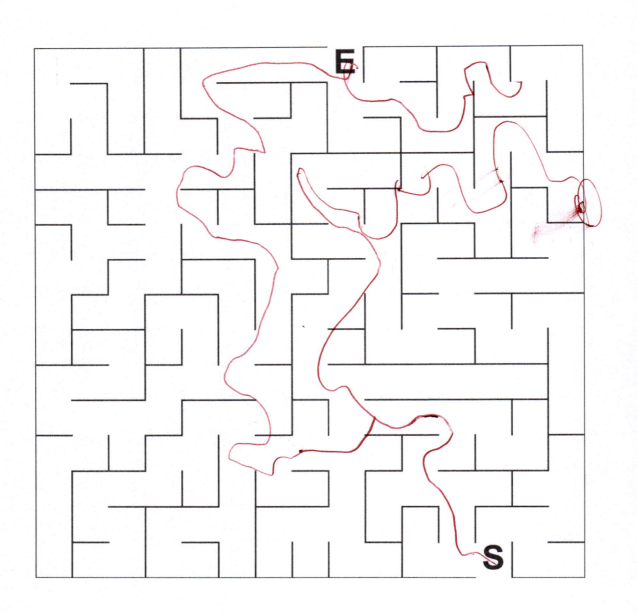

PUZZLE 37
SERIOUS

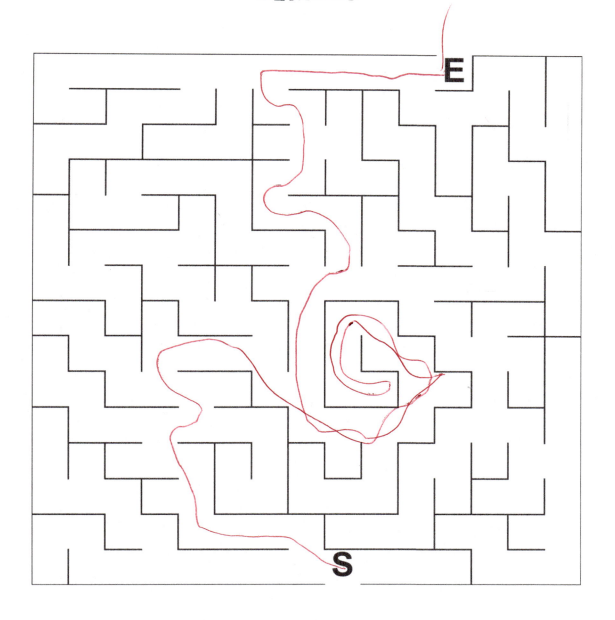

PUZZLE 38
SERIOUS

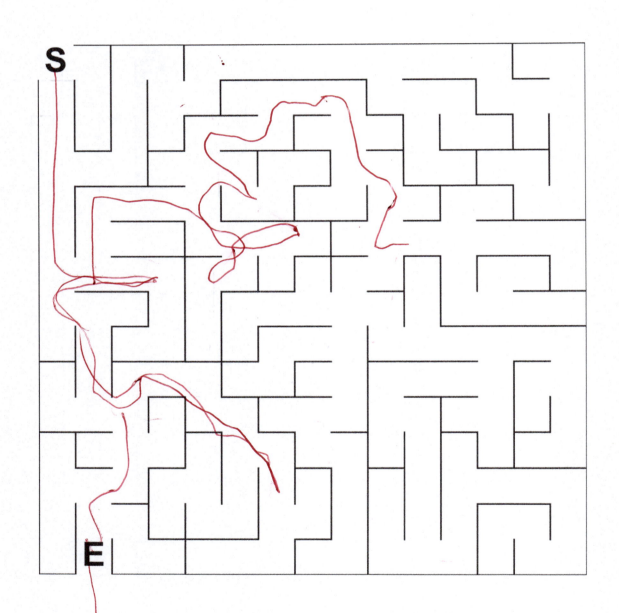

PUZZLE 39
SERIOUS

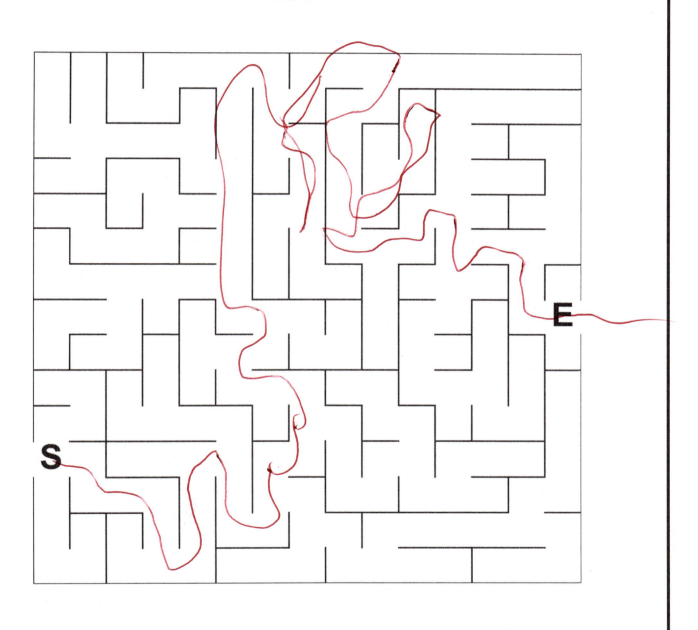

PUZZLE 40
SERIOUS

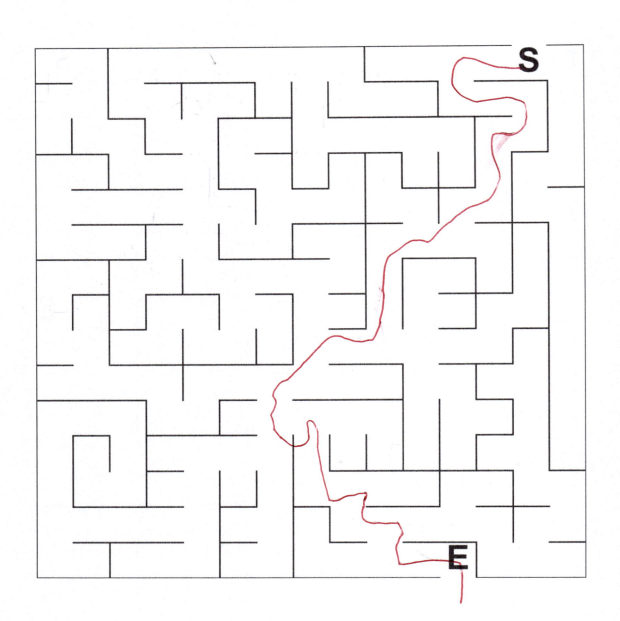

PUZZLE 41
SERIOUS

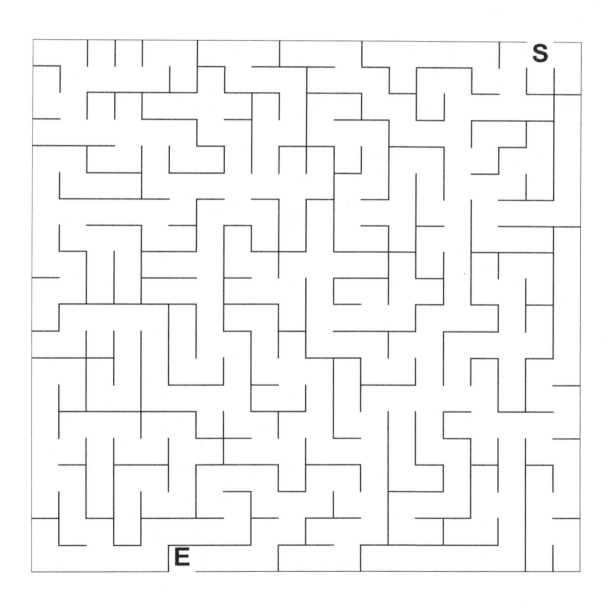

PUZZLE 42
SERIOUS

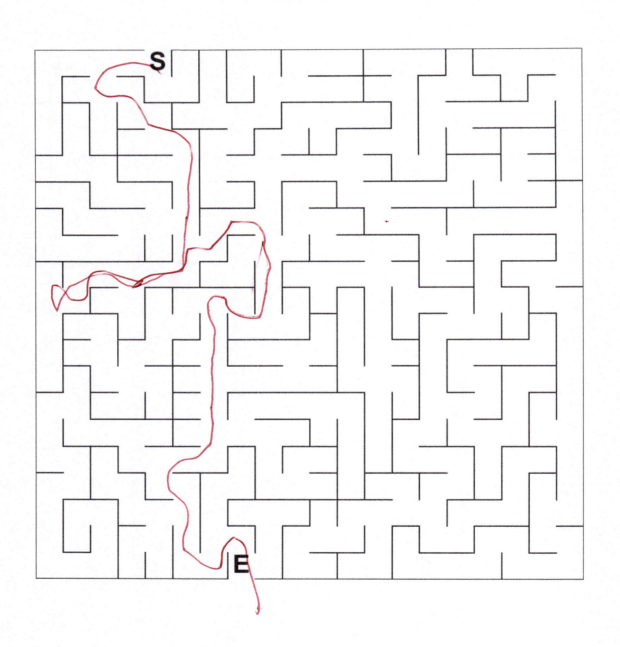

PUZZLE 43
SERIOUS

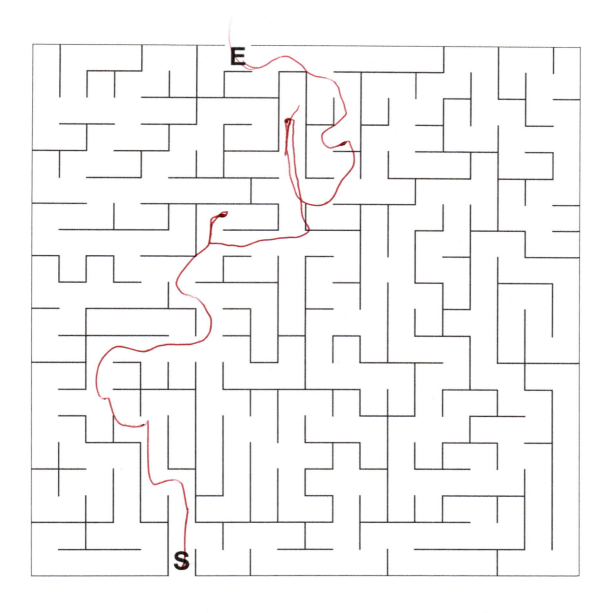

PUZZLE 44
SERIOUS

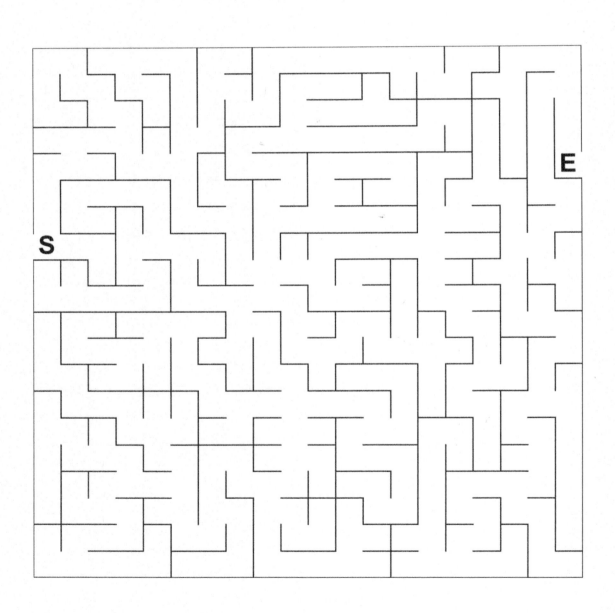

PUZZLE 45
SERIOUS

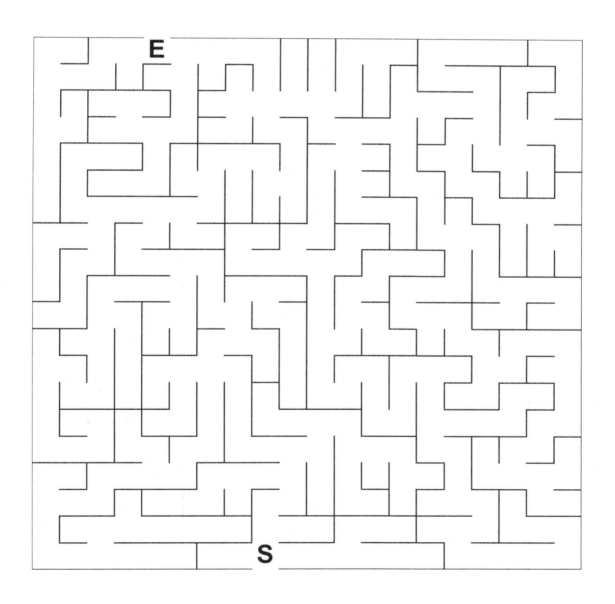

PUZZLE 46
SERIOUS

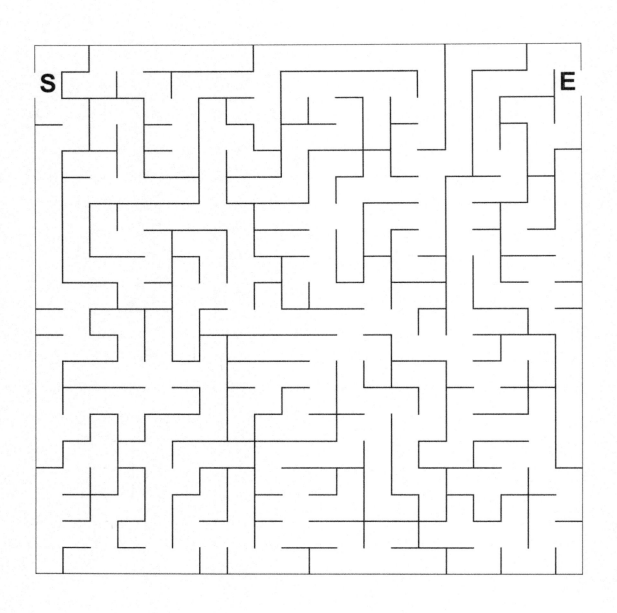

PUZZLE 47
SERIOUS

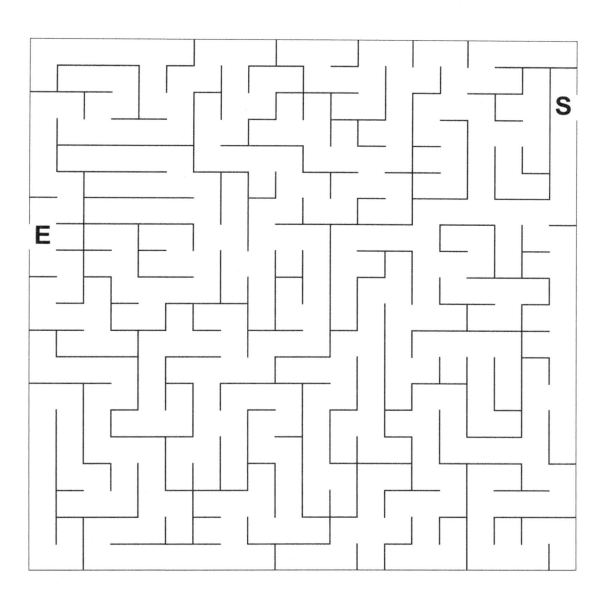

PUZZLE 48
SERIOUS

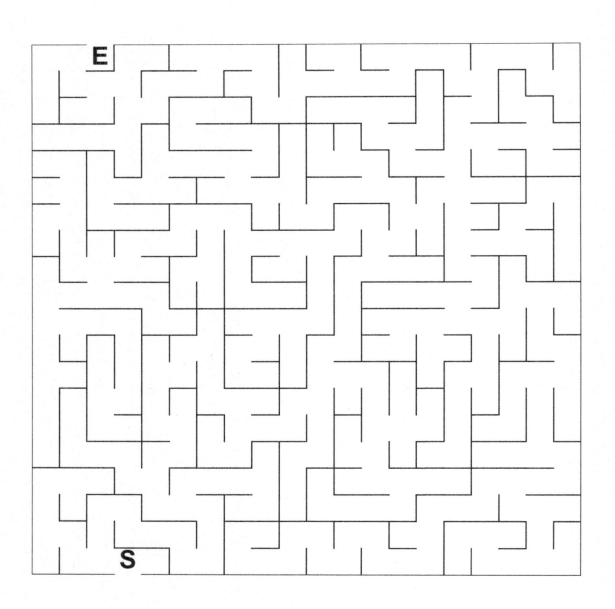

PUZZLE 49
SERIOUS

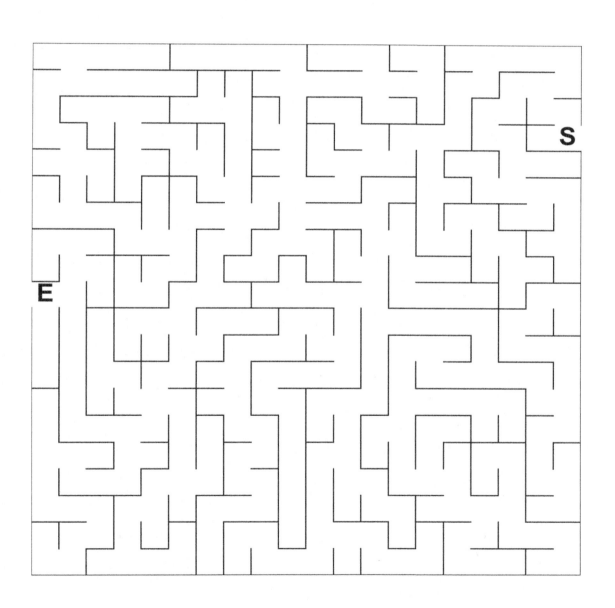

PUZZLE 50
SERIOUS

PUZZLE 51
SERIOUS

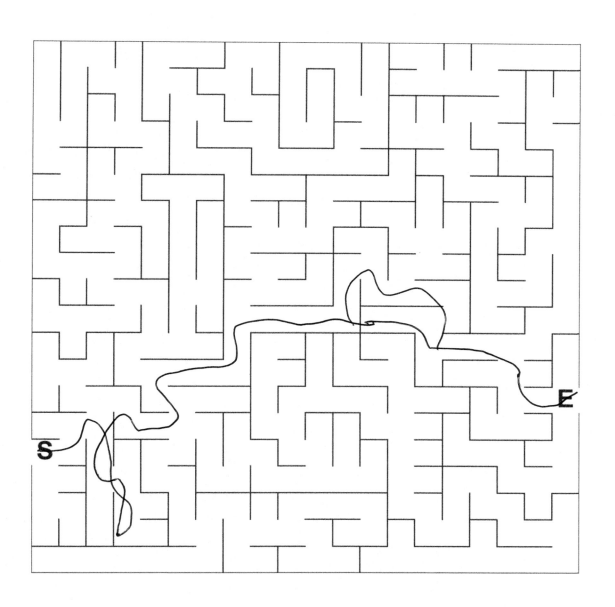

PUZZLE 52
SERIOUS

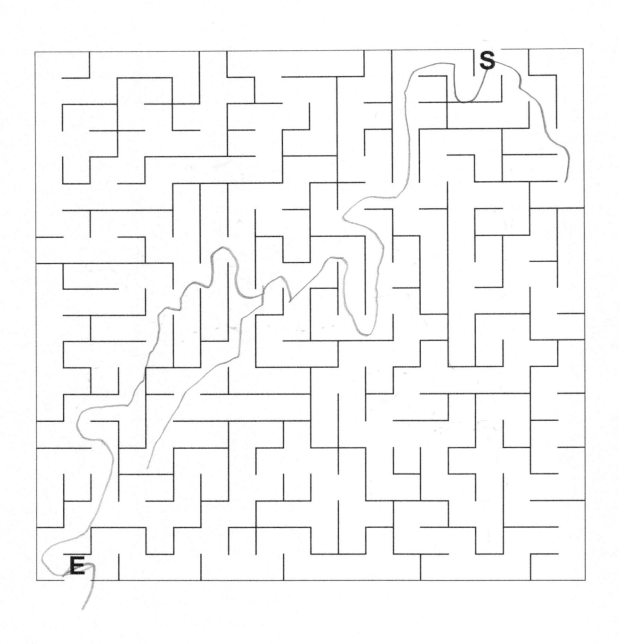

PUZZLE 53
SERIOUS

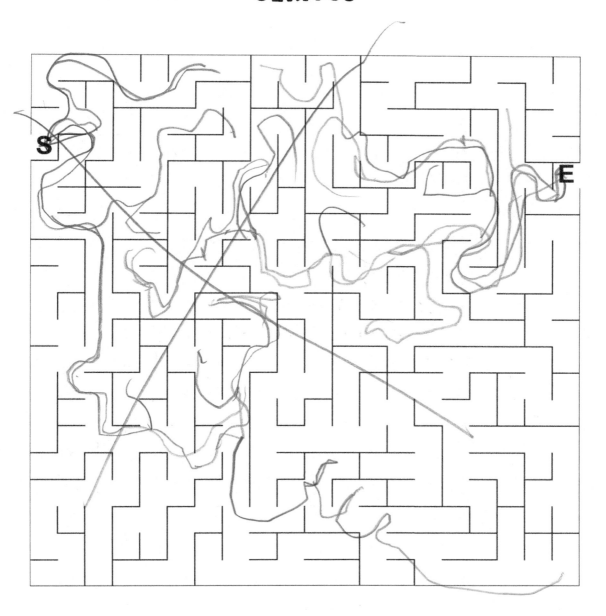

PUZZLE 54
SERIOUS

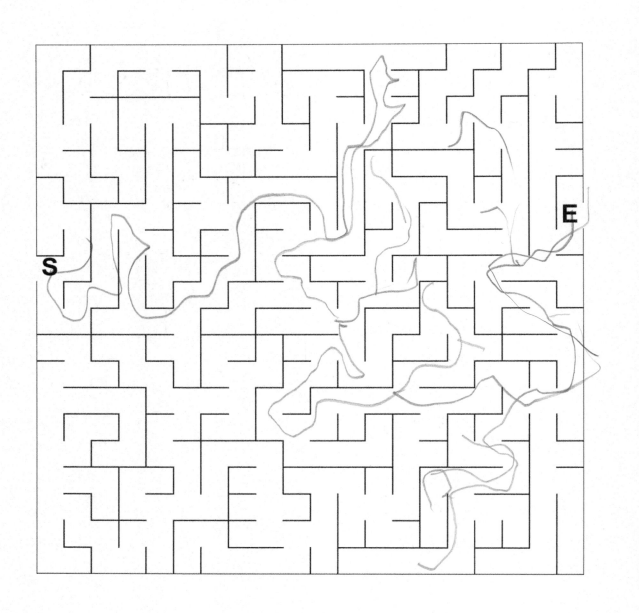

PUZZLE 55
SERIOUS

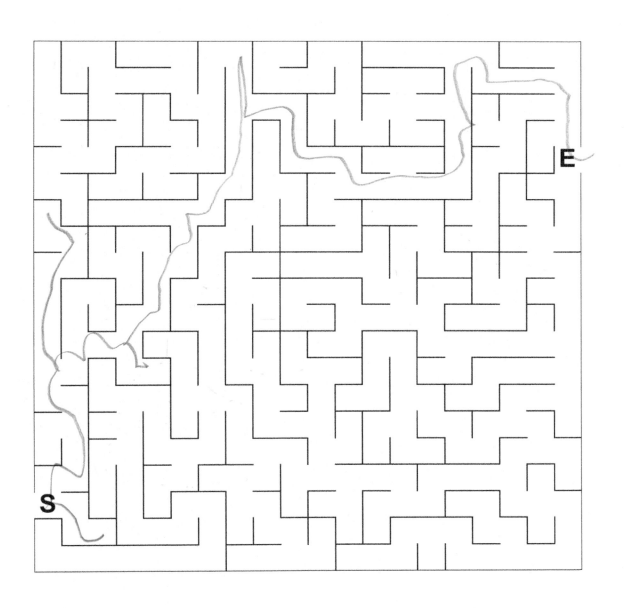

PUZZLE 56
SERIOUS

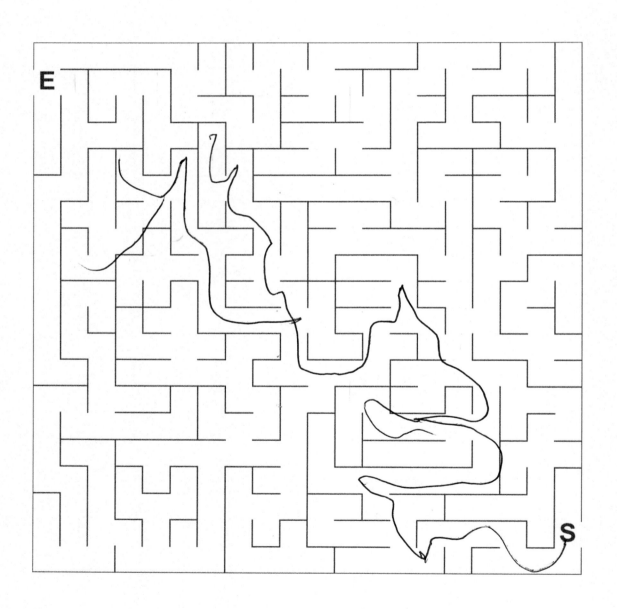

PUZZLE 57
SERIOUS

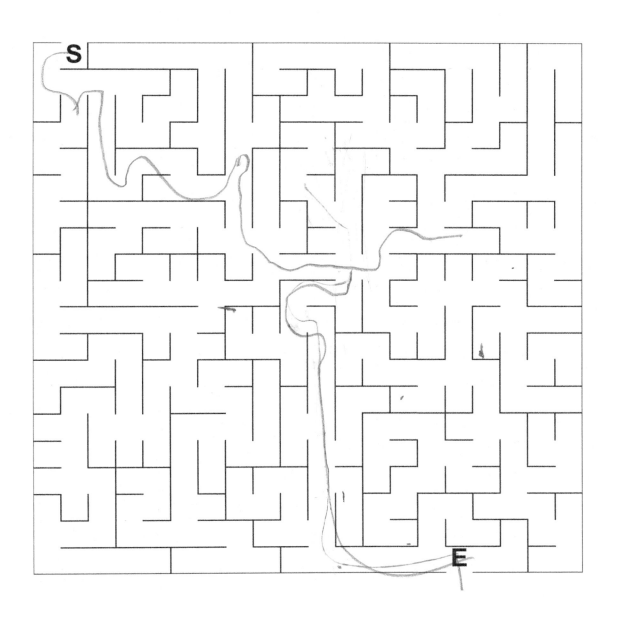

PUZZLE 58
SERIOUS

PUZZLE 60
SERIOUS

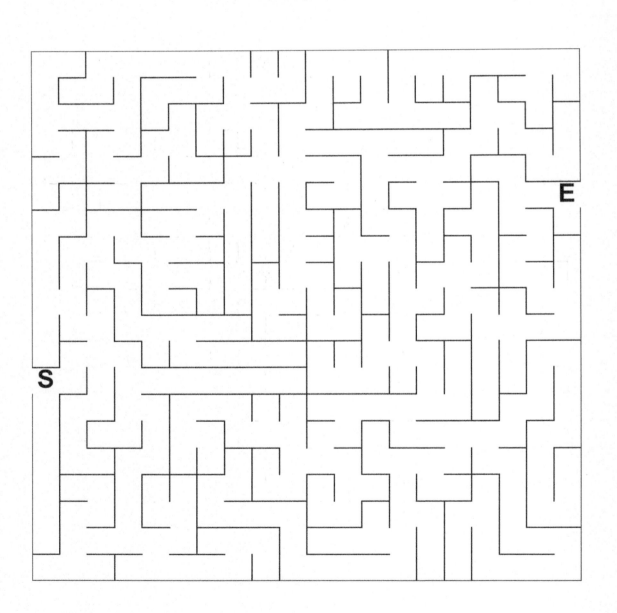

PUZZLE 61
SERIOUS

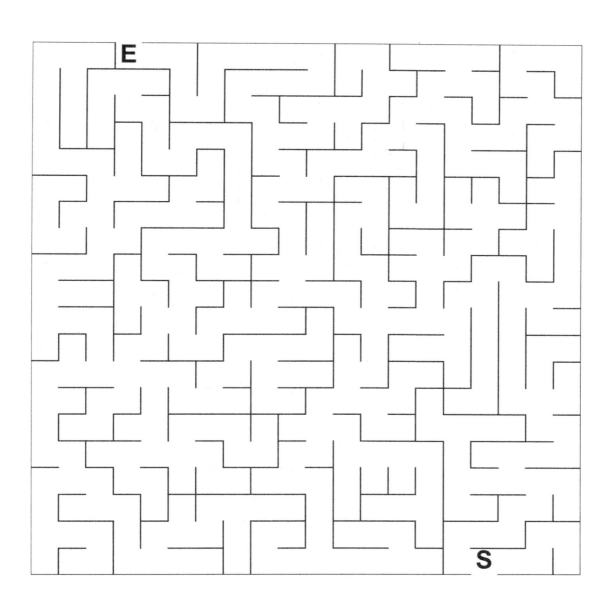

15 crushes

PUZZLE 62
SERIOUS

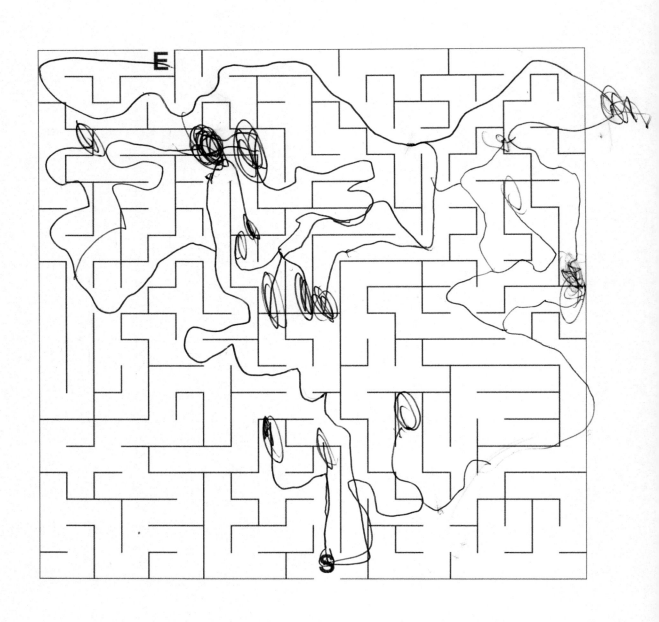

PUZZLE 63
SERIOUS

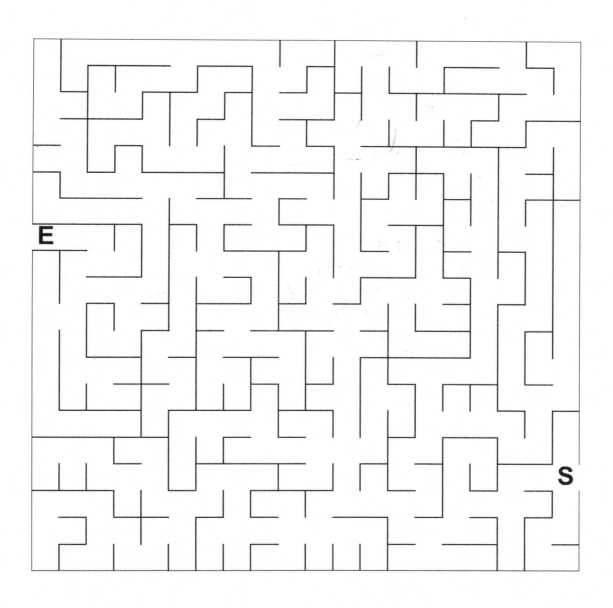

8 crossings

PUZZLE 64
SERIOUS

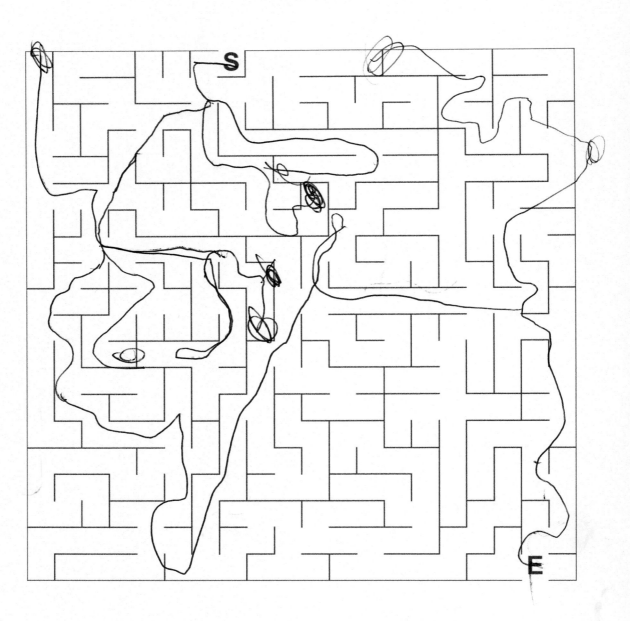

PUZZLE 65
SERIOUS

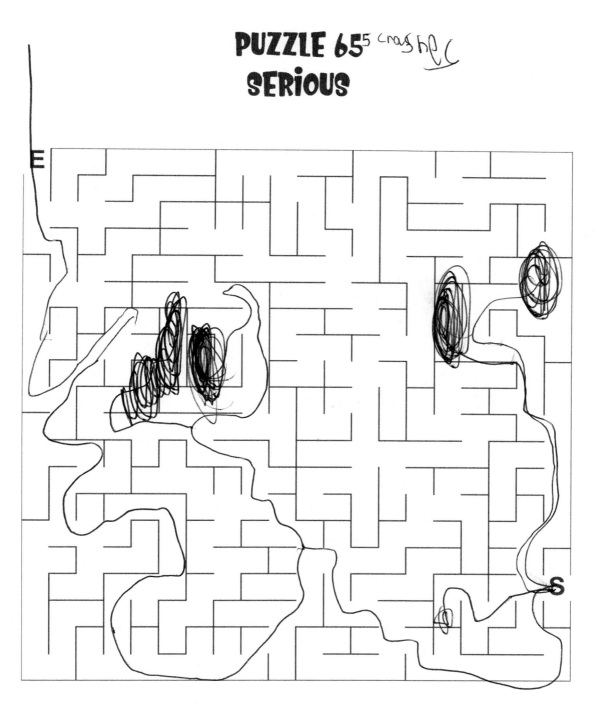

PUZZLE 66
SERIOUS

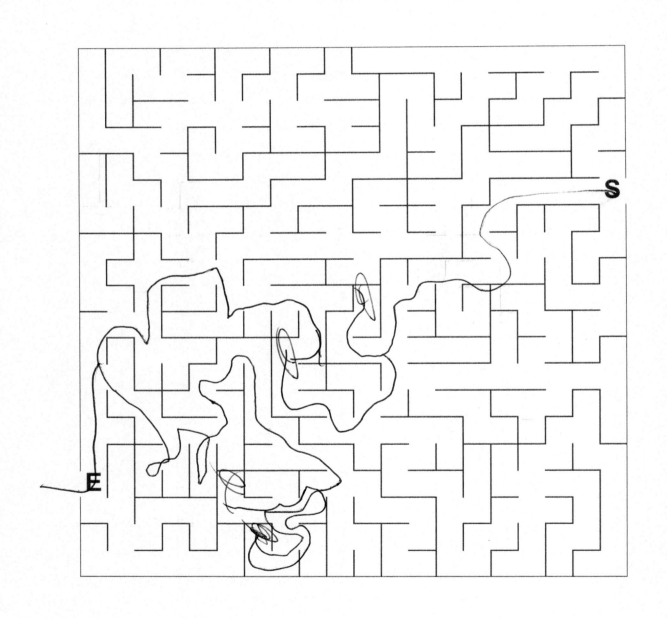

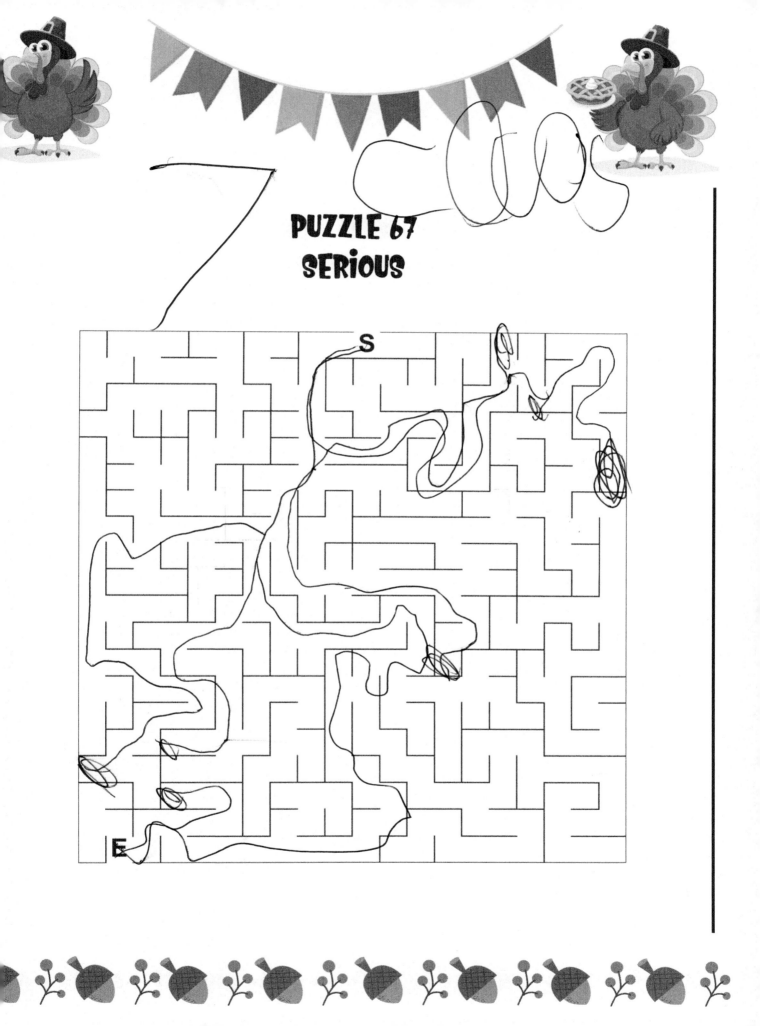

PUZZLE 68
SERIOUS

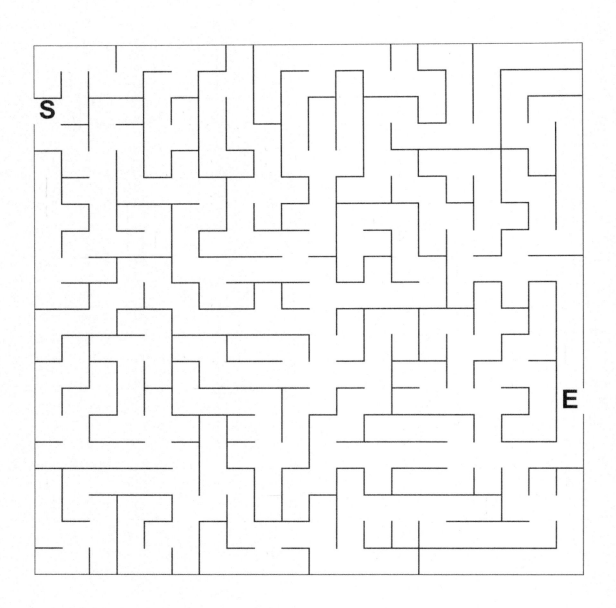

PUZZLE 69
SERIOUS

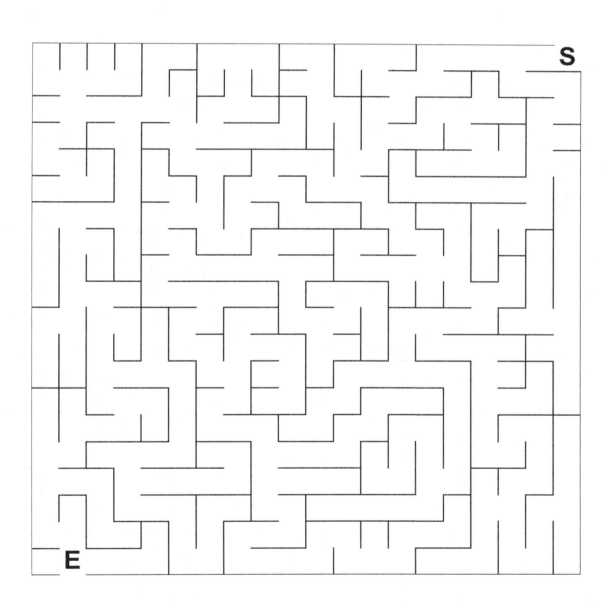

PUZZLE 70
SERIOUS

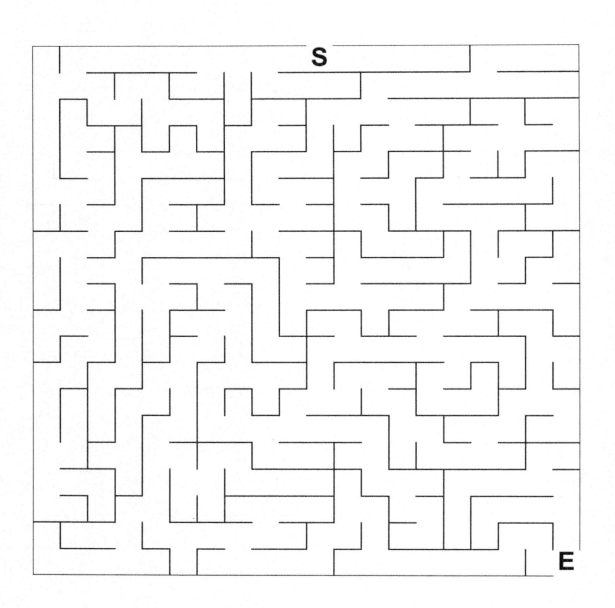

PUZZLE 71
SERIOUS

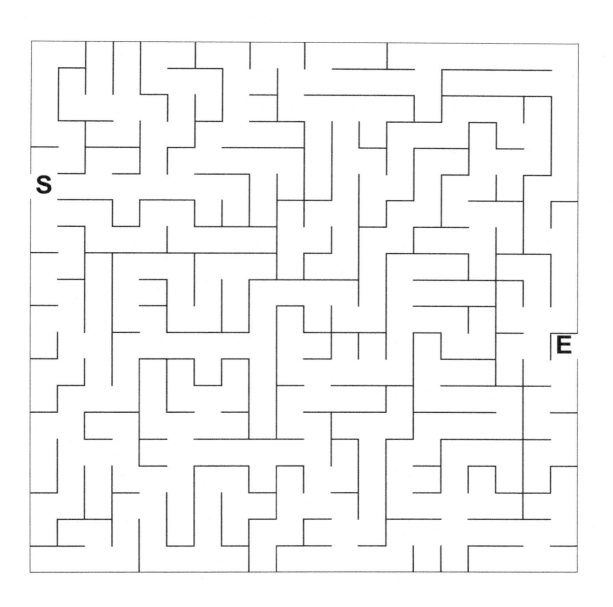

PUZZLE 72
SERIOUS

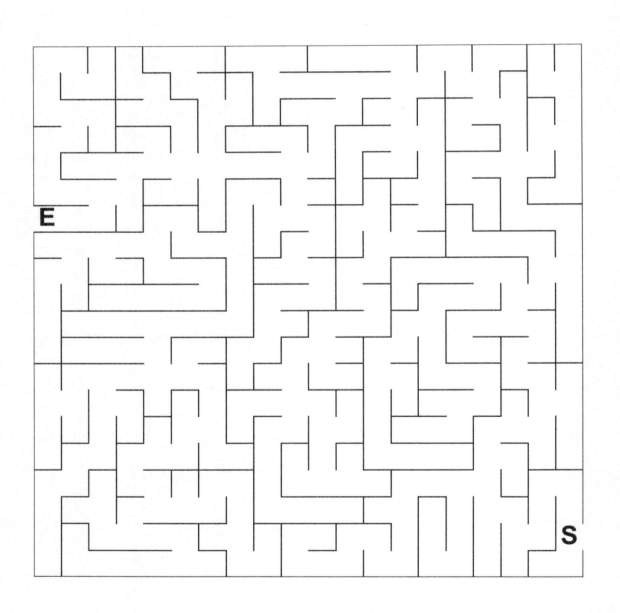

PUZZLE 73
SERIOUS

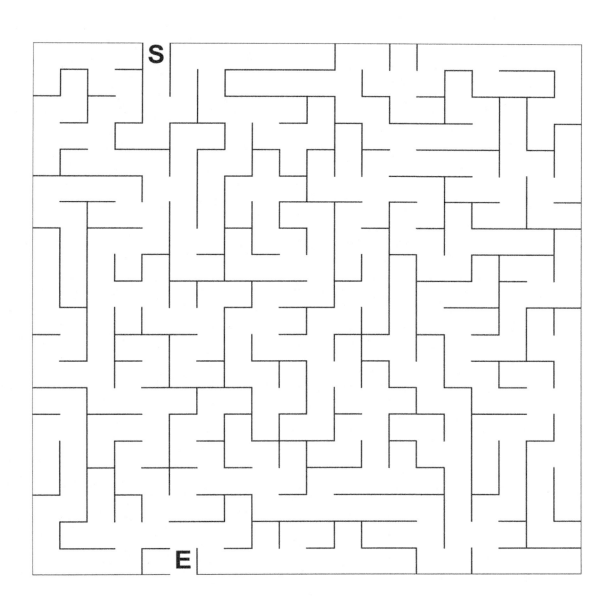

PUZZLE 74
SERIOUS

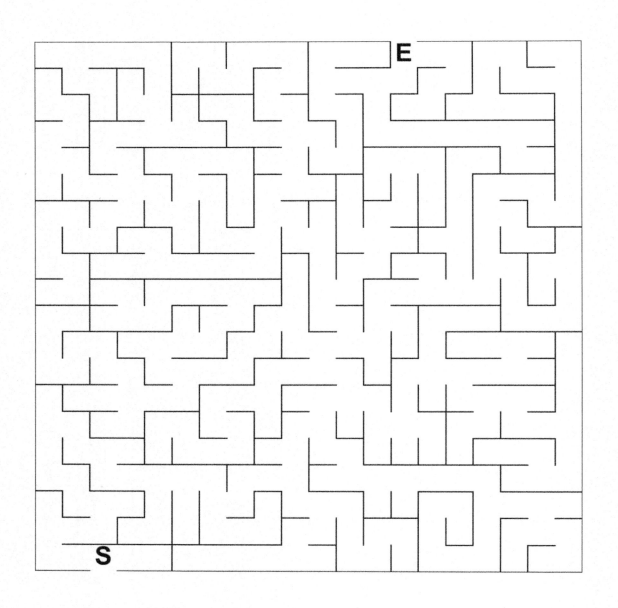

PUZZLE 75
SERIOUS

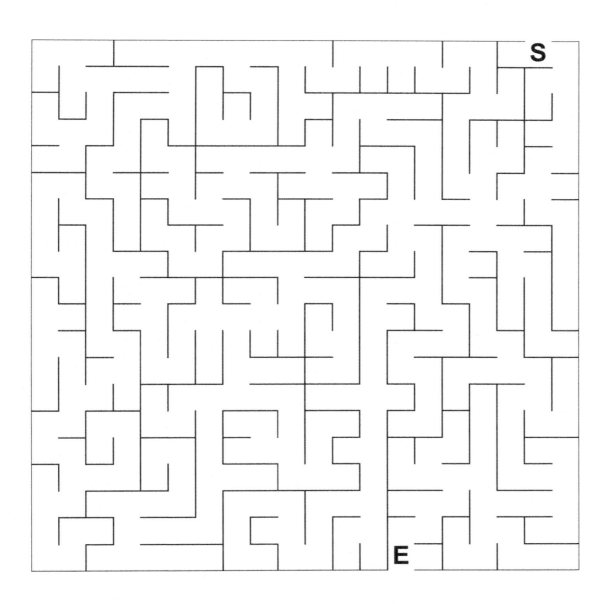

PUZZLE 76
SERIOUS

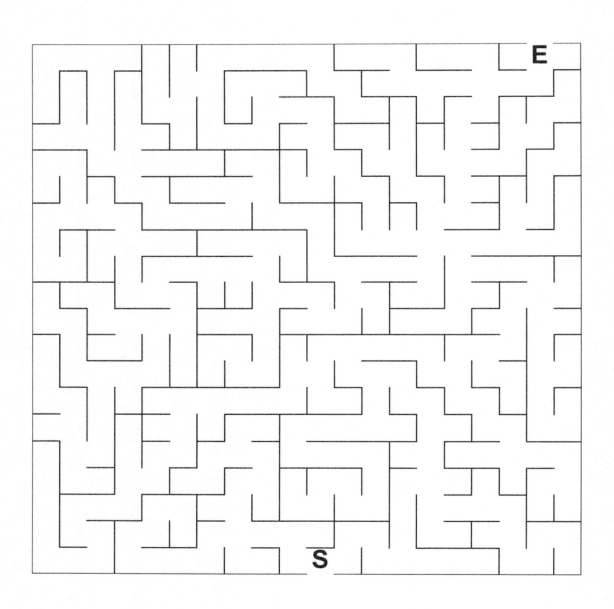

PUZZLE 77
SERIOUS

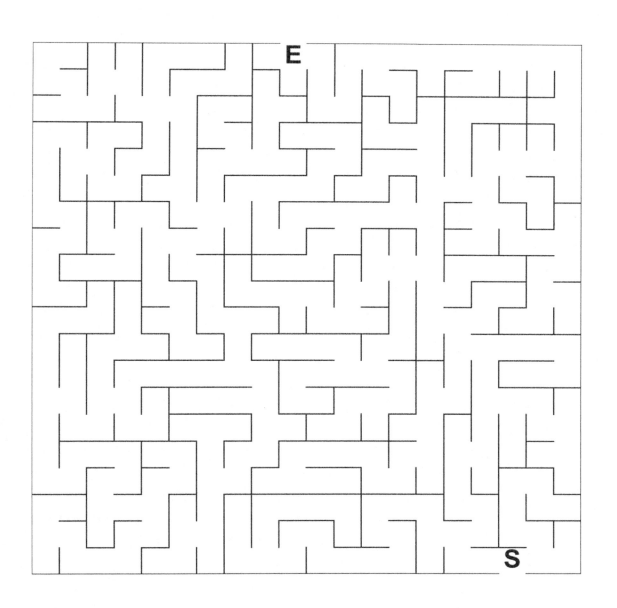

PUZZLE 78
SERIOUS

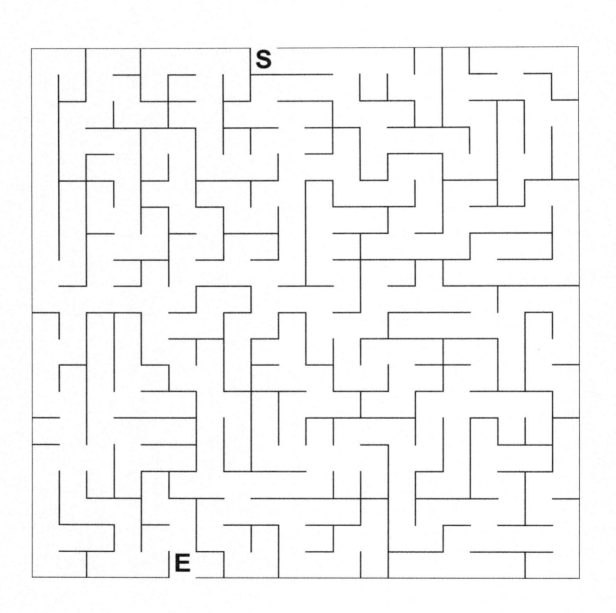

PUZZLE 79
SERIOUS

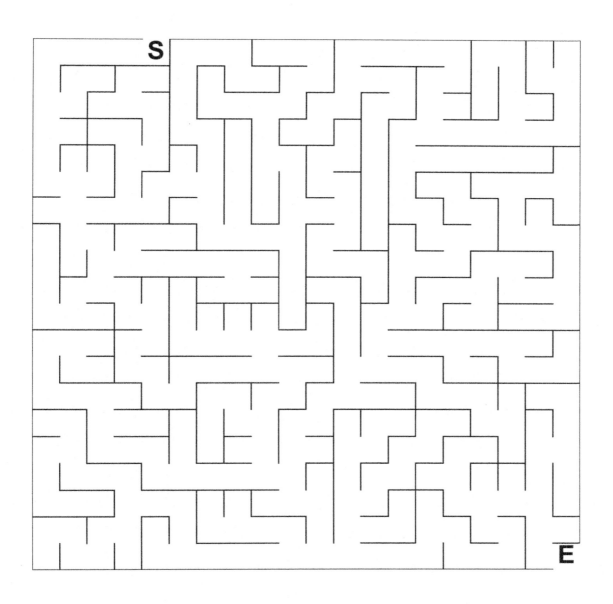

PUZZLE 80
SERIOUS

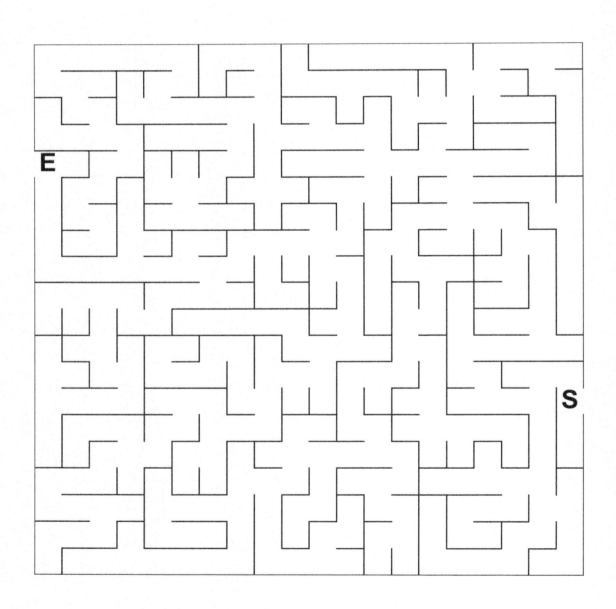

PUZZLE 81
HARD

PUZZLE 82
HARD

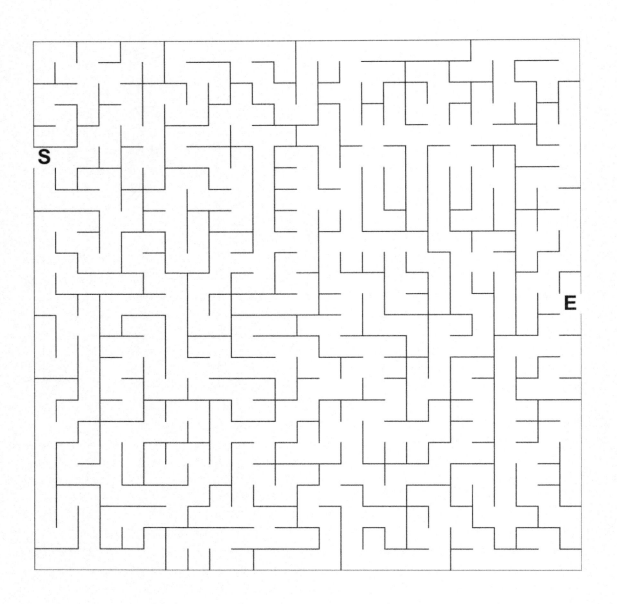

PUZZLE 83
HARD

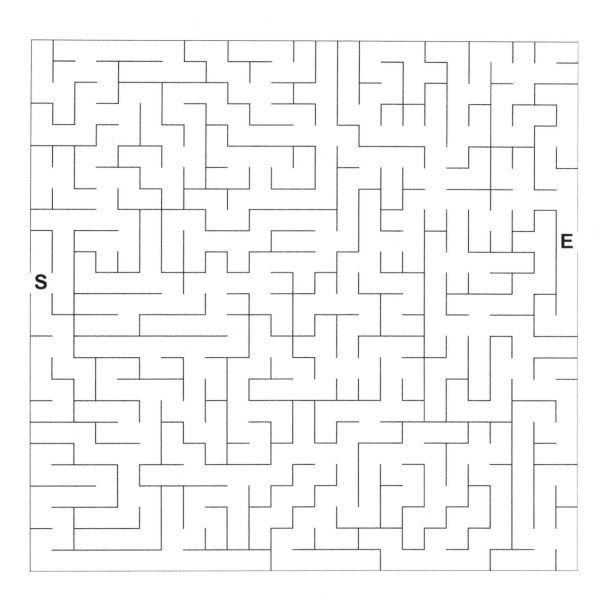

PUZZLE 84
HARD

PUZZLE 97
HARD

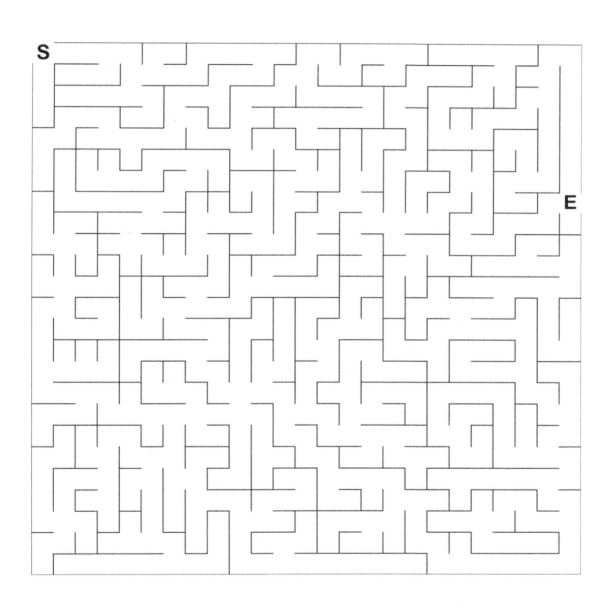

PUZZLE 98
HARD

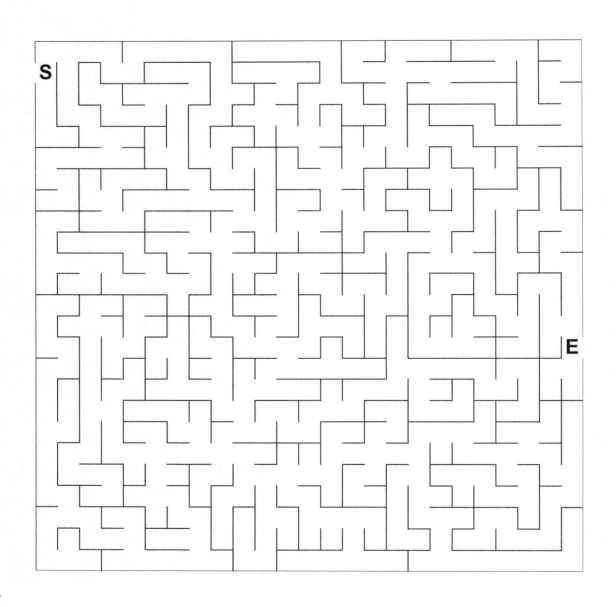

PUZZLE 99
HARD

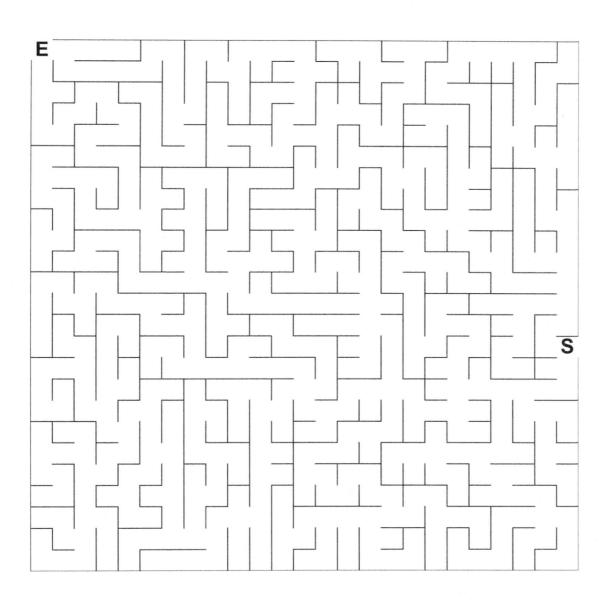

PUZZLE 100
HARD

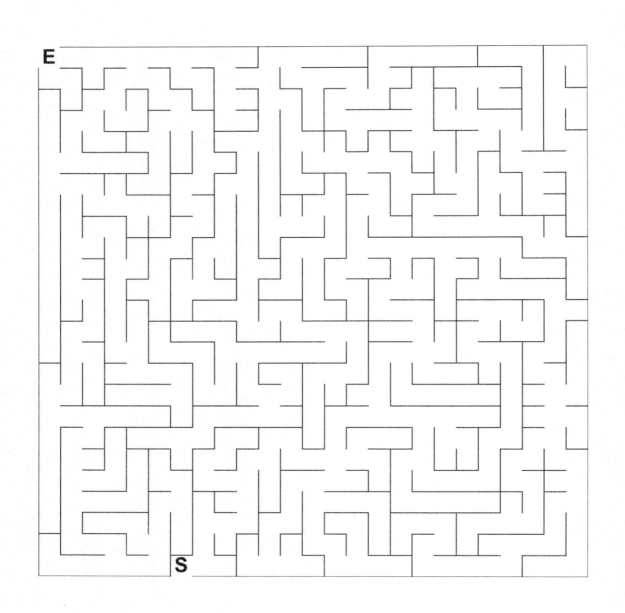

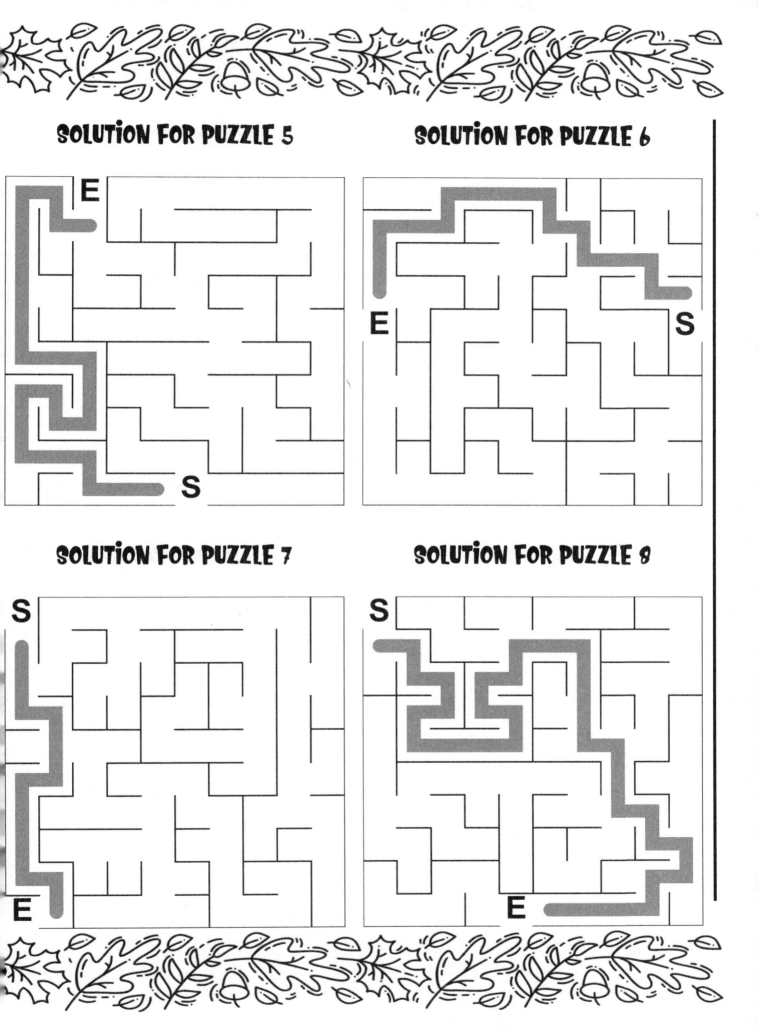

SOLUTION FOR PUZZLE 9

SOLUTION FOR PUZZLE 10

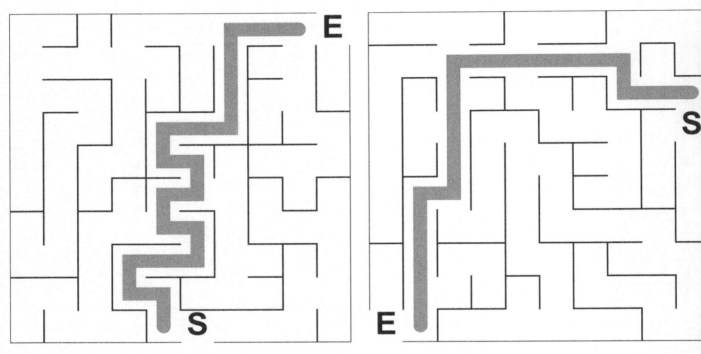

SOLUTION FOR PUZZLE 11

SOLUTION FOR PUZZLE 12

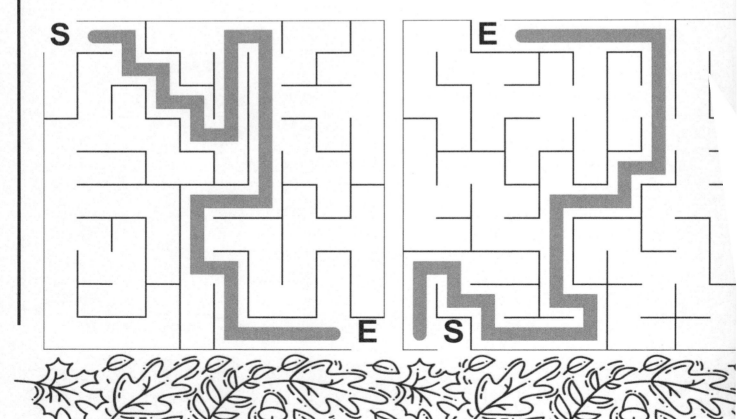

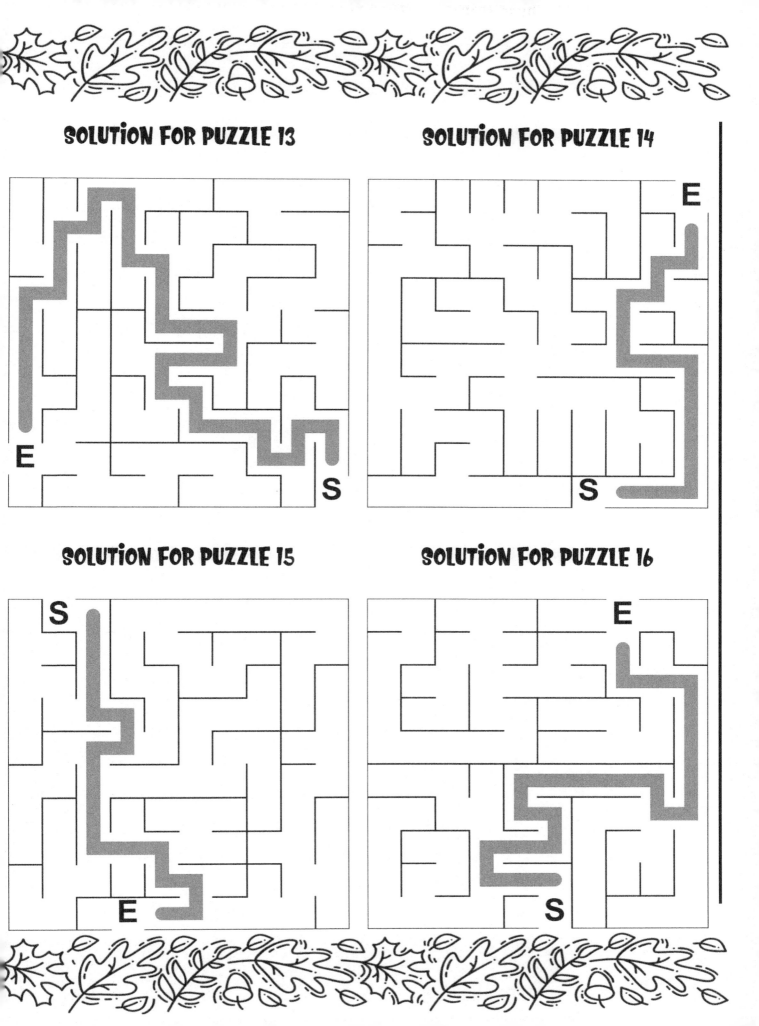

SOLUTION FOR PUZZLE 17

SOLUTION FOR PUZZLE 18

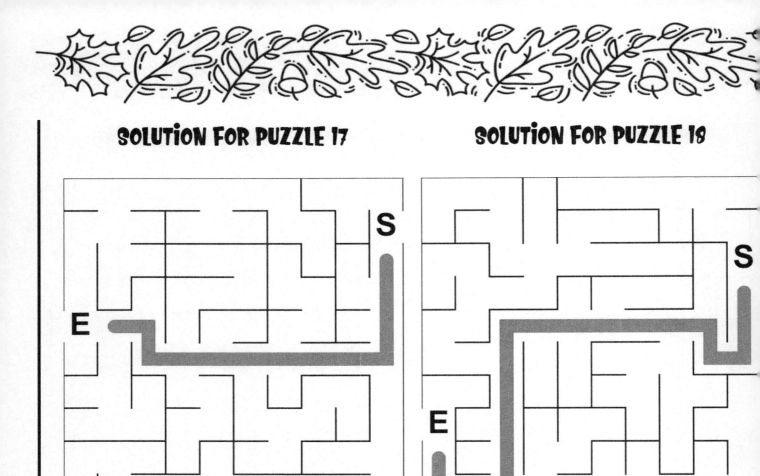

SOLUTION FOR PUZZLE 19

SOLUTION FOR PUZZLE 20

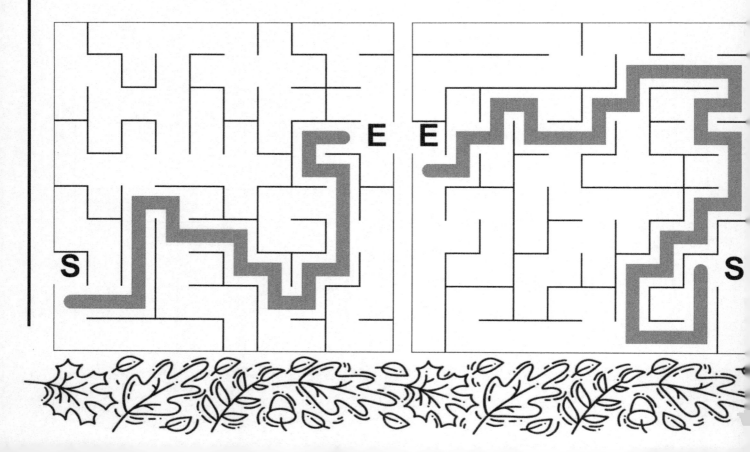

SOLUTION FOR PUZZLE 21

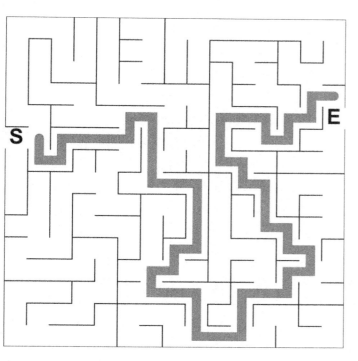

SOLUTION FOR PUZZLE 22

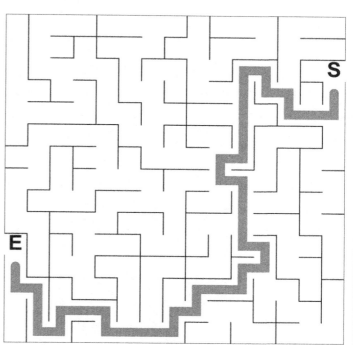

SOLUTION FOR PUZZLE 23

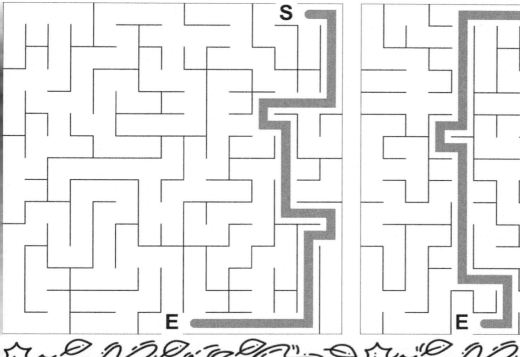

SOLUTION FOR PUZZLE 24

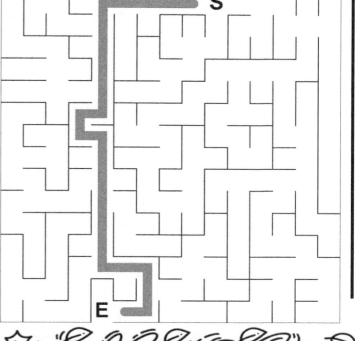

SOLUTION FOR PUZZLE 25

SOLUTION FOR PUZZLE 26

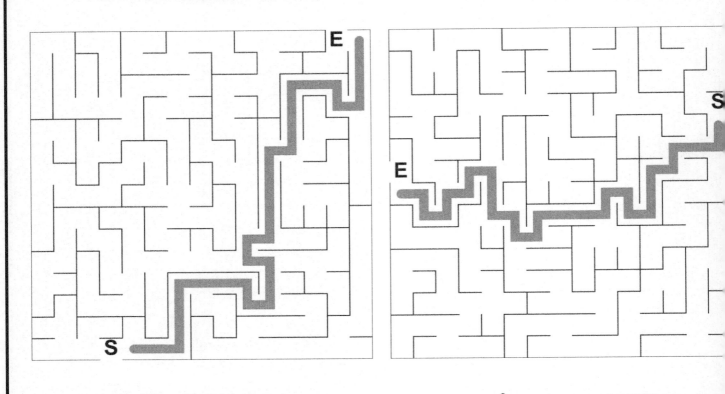

SOLUTION FOR PUZZLE 27

SOLUTION FOR PUZZLE 28

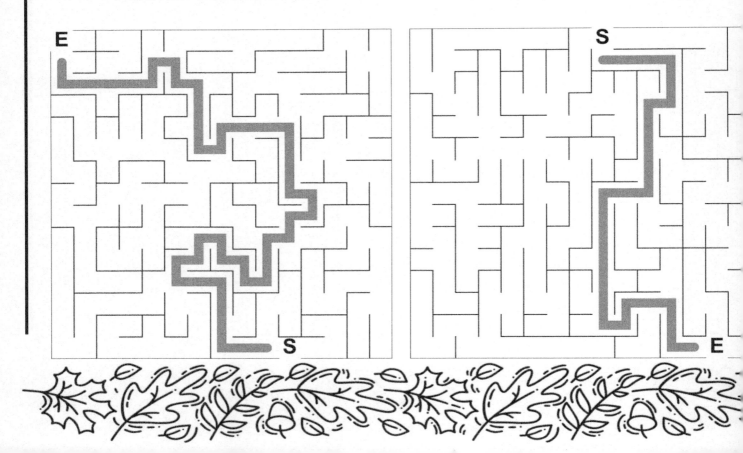

SOLUTION FOR PUZZLE 29

SOLUTION FOR PUZZLE 30

SOLUTION FOR PUZZLE 31

SOLUTION FOR PUZZLE 32

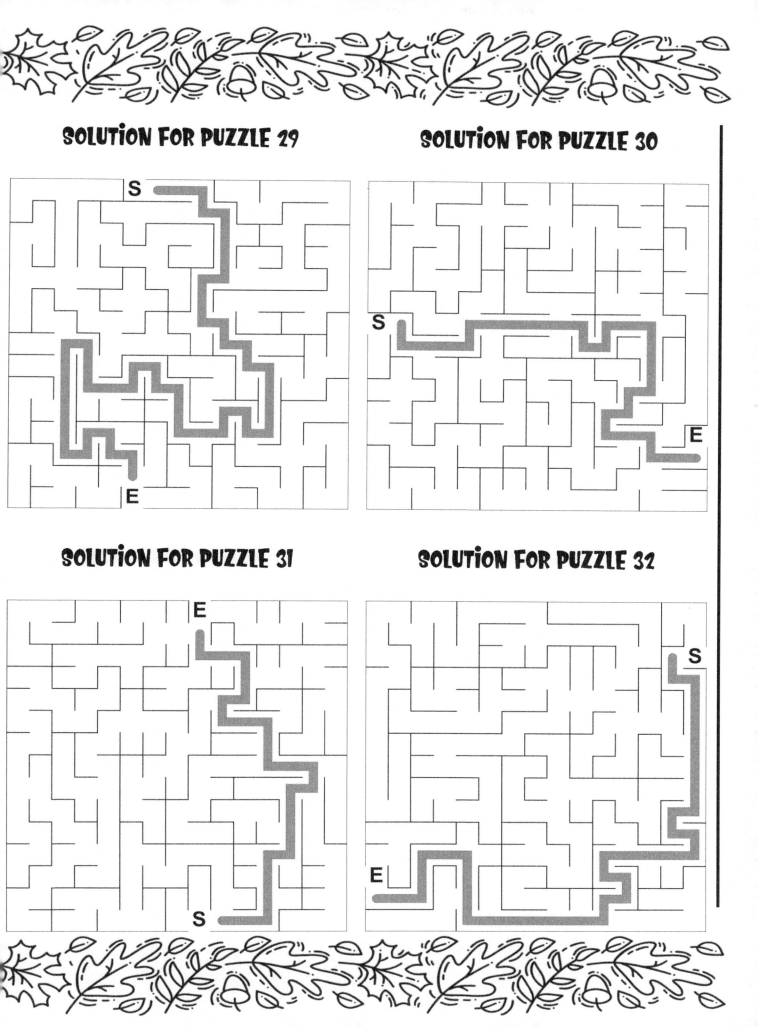

SOLUTION FOR PUZZLE 33

SOLUTION FOR PUZZLE 34

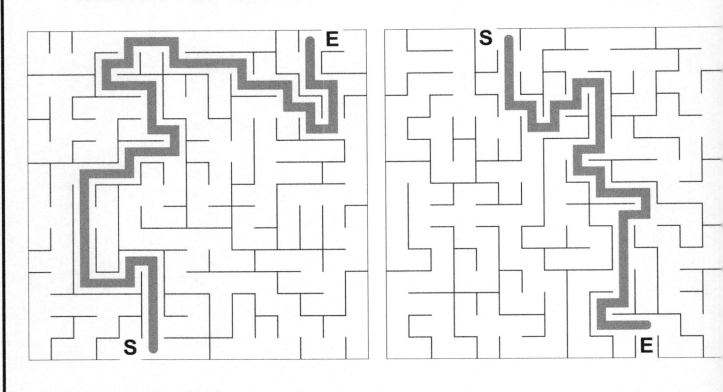

SOLUTION FOR PUZZLE 35

SOLUTION FOR PUZZLE 36

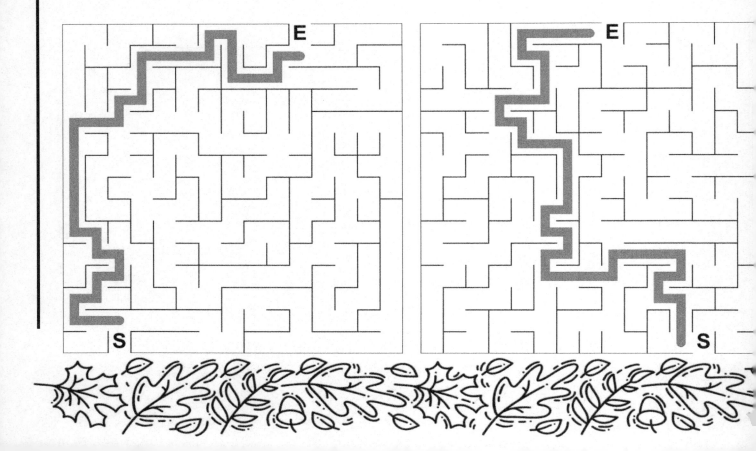

SOLUTION FOR PUZZLE 37

SOLUTION FOR PUZZLE 38

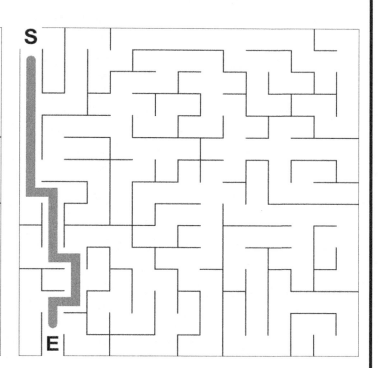

SOLUTION FOR PUZZLE 39

SOLUTION FOR PUZZLE 40

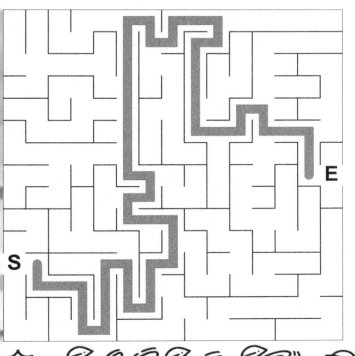
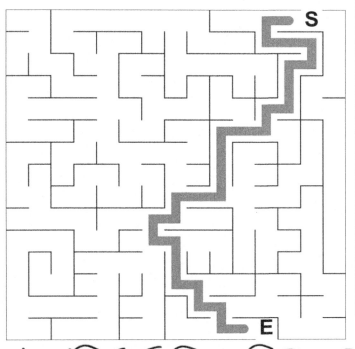

SOLUTION FOR PUZZLE 41

SOLUTION FOR PUZZLE 42

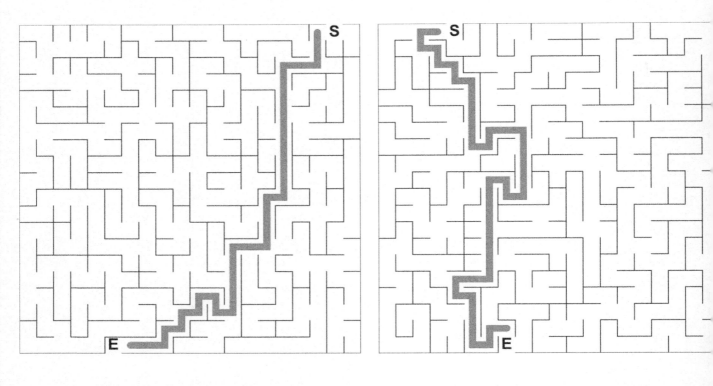

SOLUTION FOR PUZZLE 43

SOLUTION FOR PUZZLE 44

SOLUTION FOR PUZZLE 45

SOLUTION FOR PUZZLE 46

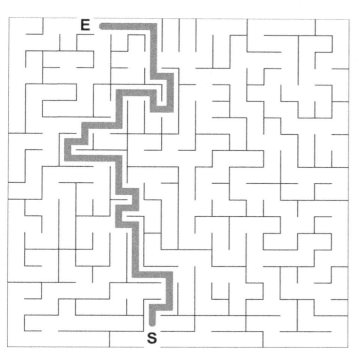
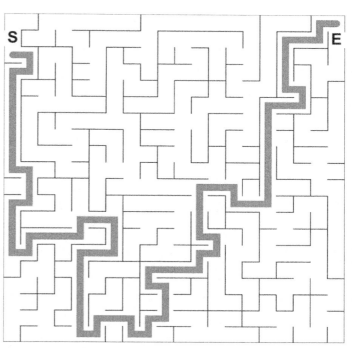

SOLUTION FOR PUZZLE 47

SOLUTION FOR PUZZLE 48

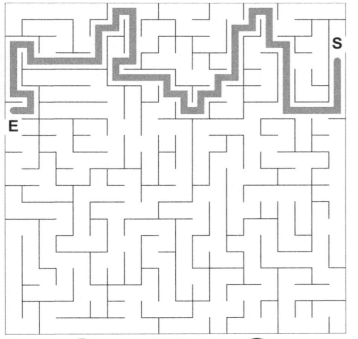
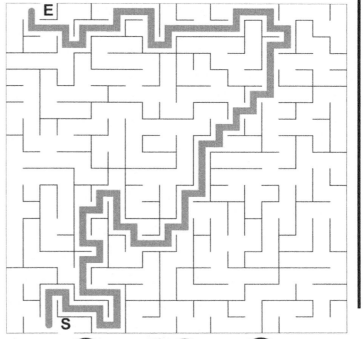

SOLUTION FOR PUZZLE 49

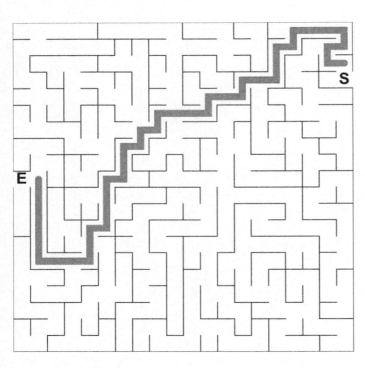

SOLUTION FOR PUZZLE 50

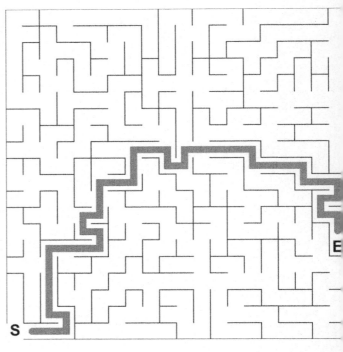

SOLUTION FOR PUZZLE 51

SOLUTION FOR PUZZLE 52

SOLUTION FOR PUZZLE 53

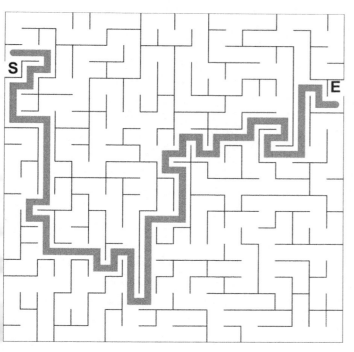

SOLUTION FOR PUZZLE 54

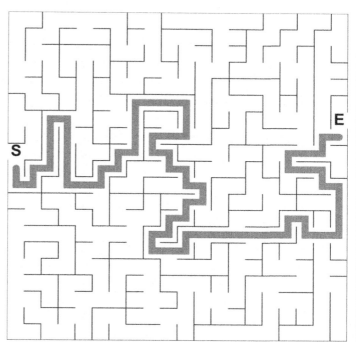

SOLUTION FOR PUZZLE 55

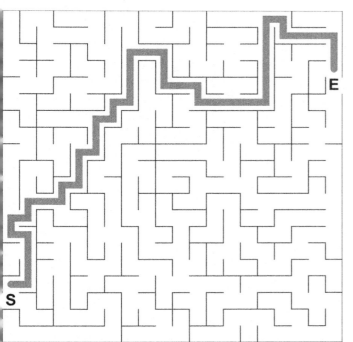

SOLUTION FOR PUZZLE 56

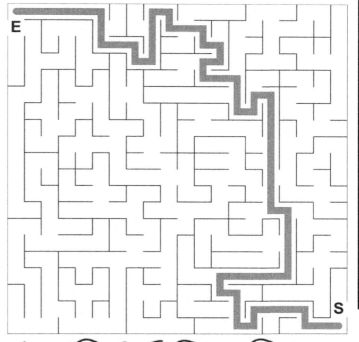

SOLUTION FOR PUZZLE 57

SOLUTION FOR PUZZLE 58

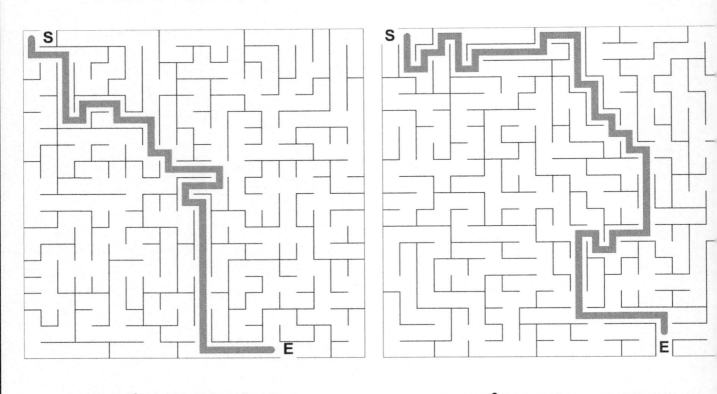

SOLUTION FOR PUZZLE 59

SOLUTION FOR PUZZLE 60

SOLUTION FOR PUZZLE 61

SOLUTION FOR PUZZLE 62

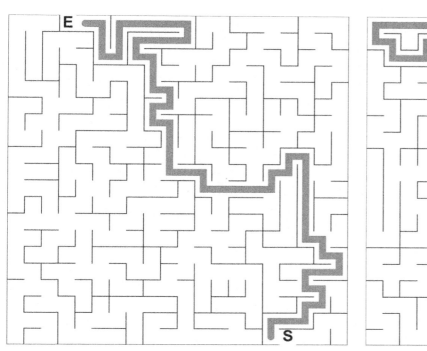
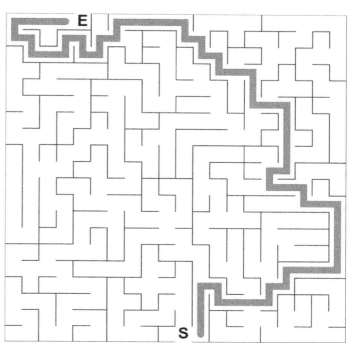

SOLUTION FOR PUZZLE 63

SOLUTION FOR PUZZLE 64

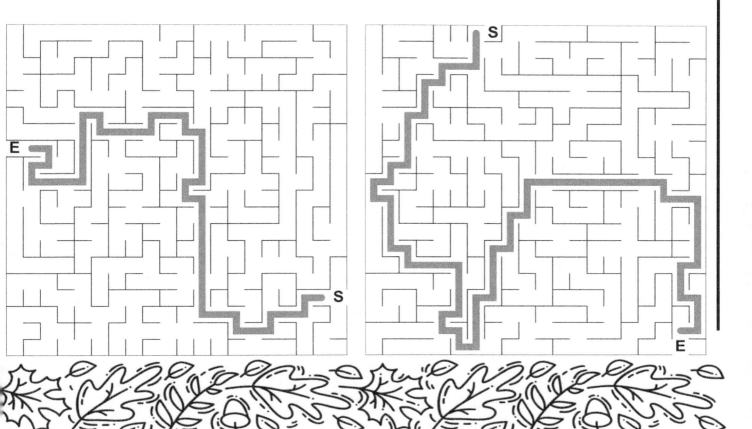

SOLUTION FOR PUZZLE 65

SOLUTION FOR PUZZLE 66

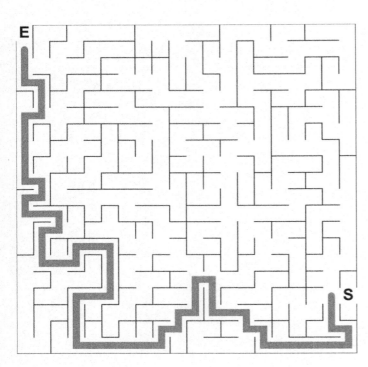
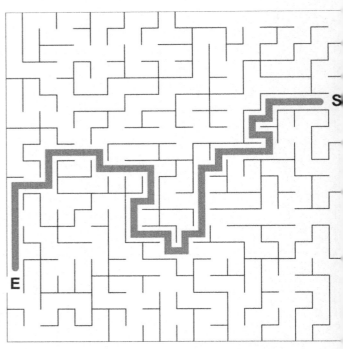

SOLUTION FOR PUZZLE 67

SOLUTION FOR PUZZLE 68

SOLUTION FOR PUZZLE 69

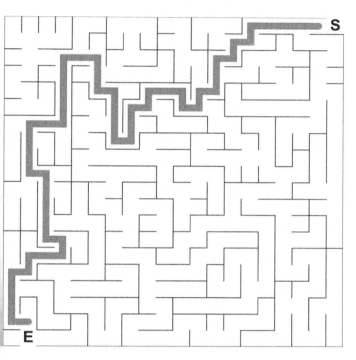

SOLUTION FOR PUZZLE 70

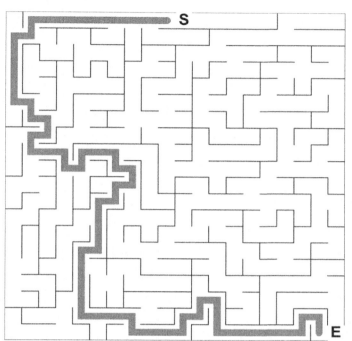

SOLUTION FOR PUZZLE 71

SOLUTION FOR PUZZLE 72

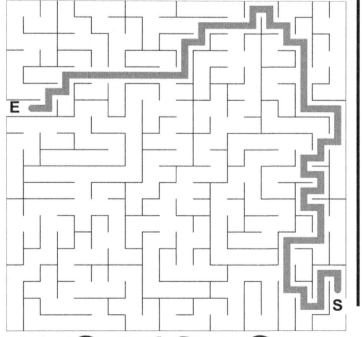

SOLUTION FOR PUZZLE 73

SOLUTION FOR PUZZLE 74

SOLUTION FOR PUZZLE 75

SOLUTION FOR PUZZLE 76

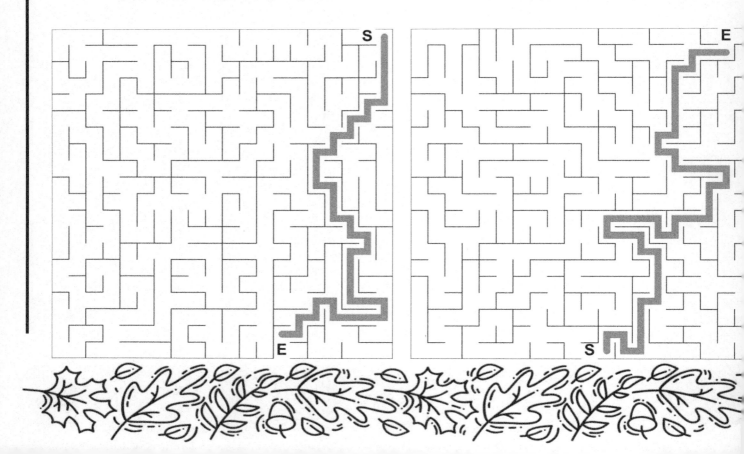

SOLUTION FOR PUZZLE 77

SOLUTION FOR PUZZLE 78

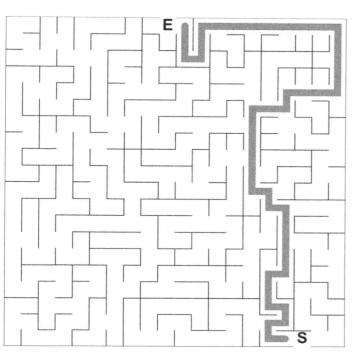
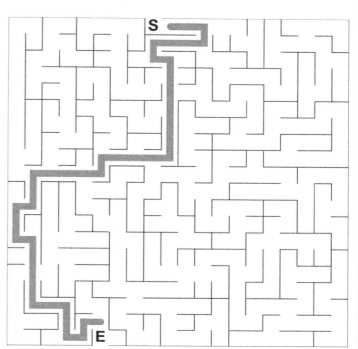

SOLUTION FOR PUZZLE 79

SOLUTION FOR PUZZLE 80

SOLUTION FOR PUZZLE 81

SOLUTION FOR PUZZLE 82

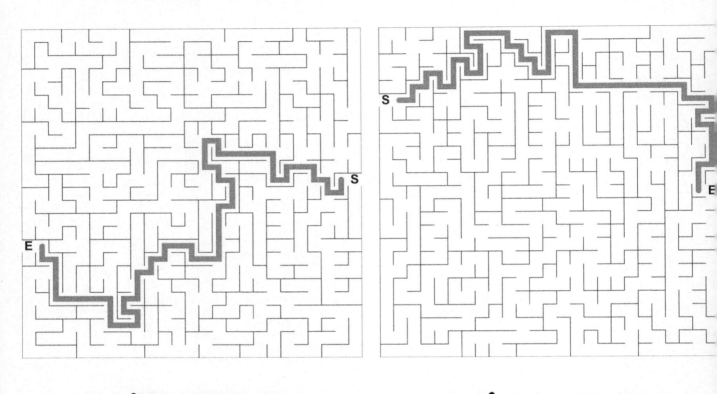

SOLUTION FOR PUZZLE 83

SOLUTION FOR PUZZLE 84

SOLUTION FOR PUZZLE 85

SOLUTION FOR PUZZLE 86

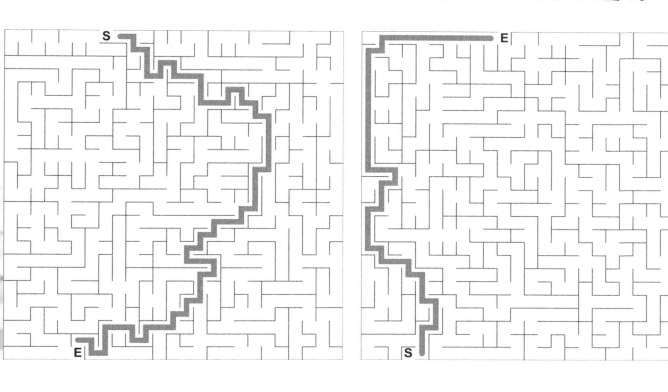

SOLUTION FOR PUZZLE 87

SOLUTION FOR PUZZLE 88

SOLUTION FOR PUZZLE 89

SOLUTION FOR PUZZLE 90

SOLUTION FOR PUZZLE 91

SOLUTION FOR PUZZLE 92

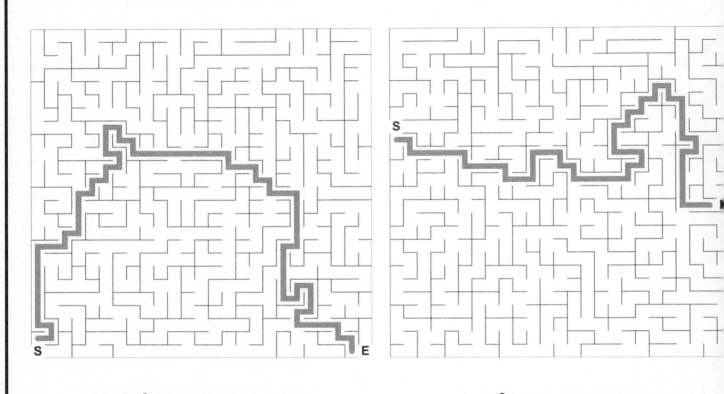

SOLUTION FOR PUZZLE 93

SOLUTION FOR PUZZLE 94

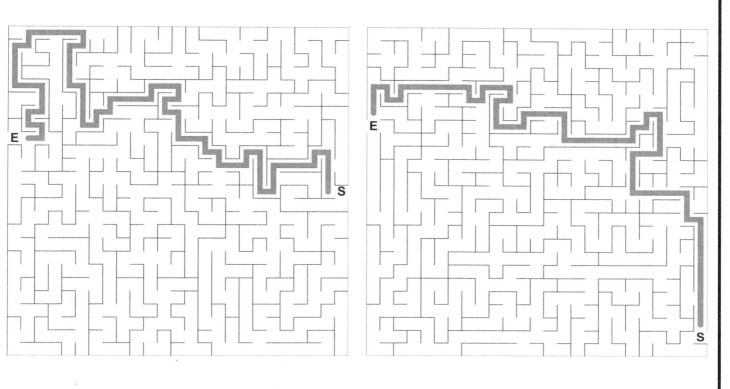

SOLUTION FOR PUZZLE 95

SOLUTION FOR PUZZLE 96

SOLUTION FOR PUZZLE 97

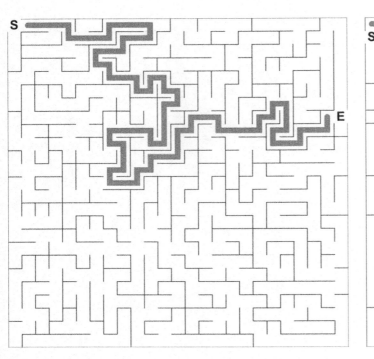

SOLUTION FOR PUZZLE 98

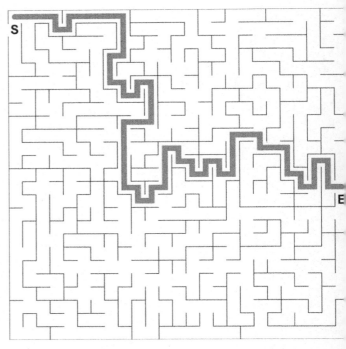

SOLUTION FOR PUZZLE 99

SOLUTION FOR PUZZLE 100

SOLUTION FOR PUZZLE 101

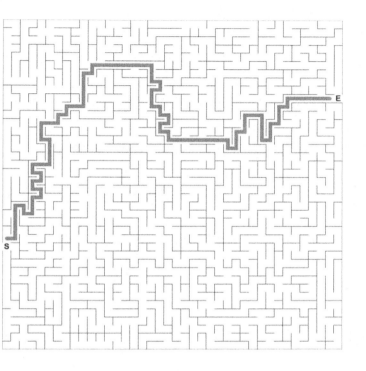

Printed in Great Britain
by Amazon